I0880598

No Work Finished Here

No Work Finished Here

Rewriting Andy Warhol

Liz Worth

BookThug 2015

FIRST EDITION

Canada Council for the Arts | Conseil des Arts du Canada

Financé par le gouvernement du Canada | Funded by the Government of Canada | Canada

ONTARIO ARTS COUNCIL
CONSEIL DES ARTS DE L'ONTARIO
an Ontario government agency
un organisme du gouvernement de l'Ontario

The production of this book was made possible through the generous assistance of the Canada Council for the Arts and the Ontario Arts Council. BookThug also acknowledges the support of the Government of Canada through the Canada Book Fund and the Government of Ontario through the Ontario Book Publishing Tax Credit and the Ontario Book Fund.

LIBRARY AND ARCHIVES CANADA
CATALOGUING IN PUBLICATION

Worth, Liz, 1982–, author
No work finished here : rewriting Andy Warhol / Liz Worth.
—First edition.

Issued in print and electronic formats.
ISBN 978-1-77166-164-5 (PAPERBACK).–ISBN 978-1-77166-165-2 (HTML).–
ISBN 978-1-77166-166-9 (PDF).–ISBN 978-1-77166-167-6 (MOBI KINDLE)

1. Warhol, Andy, 1928–1987. A, a novel–Adaptations. I. Warhol, Andy, 1928–1987. A, a novel. II. Title.

PS8645.O767N69 2015 C811'.6 C2015-905496-6
C2015-905497-4

PRINTED IN CANADA

This one's for my dad.

You are here

I didn't do a thing last night
felt like a ghost
just staying up and all that, just talking
car noises in the background.
Some of my throat is gone.
Need some Obertrols—blue ones, blasting
oh, the orange ones are divine.

Is there ANY place we can keep calling
voice on the other end
know where we can get some.
This number in front of us—sister would know us.

We should start for the park. Takes forever.
Asleep on the bus, too gorgeous.
It's all right—fantastic, baby,
you definitely are here.

I wanted to believe this

We're going to spend this whole day
trying to find out
what I did last night.

You went to the whorehouse.
They don't have any electricity,
it's all bare skin, washed-out noises,
mean girls, roughly treated.

I hate all that. Horrid.

Maybe we should have a cup of coffee
uptown
in the park.
I wanted to believe this
business of another marvelous world but
I don't remember.
I remember we—

People aren't equipped for my filth

From the outside
there's always trouble
so precious like
living higher than
every other day.

Amuse me up here,
in background
seventy-seventh cut especially weird,
like living a riot.

I lose lots of friends and
been robbed twice,
all of my amphetamine, time.
People aren't equipped for my filth and
I can't be deceptive.
I don't know why.

Hey listen
I think we better go through everything amazing.
Why don't we take a hit,
sweet subterfuge
walk way down there.
Upset doesn't matter. Someone always loses something.

My darling

My darling got mean.
She said it was just one of those days.
I suspected television,
magnificent rumors.

I didn't have to know
the spread of wonder
would save her.

For the first time
she's afraid of what
someone said to me—
"you're really fucking her up, aren't you?"
I won't answer that.

They don't want to think of her and
last night's visit,
pressure recorded as blood.

Everyone looks so happy
as they tell me about her
pinching drugs,
working the divine to zero.
Can't support what people are believing.
She's still as night.
What do you hold? Not her.

Dare to stop us

I'm beginning to talk like her,
the girl who says she wants anything:
sleeping pills
coffee
a little mother.
Afraid somebody's gonna forget to be
vaguely interested.

I slept over last night.
She doesn't look like the same person
in the nighttime
slipping barbituates,
a mysterious act.
If she wants a drug, she takes it.
How stoned do you get
with your life in your hands?

To be a missing woman
in the morning
is to go off on your own, be a
mysterious presence, completely marvelous
cut off from names and talk and sounds.
Jolting in time to a
furious problem.

Say we had to.
Dare to stop us.

Who cares

I'm not hungry,
just chewed an
enormous flower of
bubble gum.

I'm being snubbed
at the counter,
an old friend out of season.
Do you know what it feels like?

Just slap me in the face.
I don't understand the
private booth, wonder
when they'll crawl out.
Such a fool, to walk
down the street,
meet people—please.

I always say who cares
but the letter is a gallery
of wonder,
fresh noise
on this side of loved.

I don't think he saw me.

I don't think he was taken
with who I am.

I go under like a wonderful third time

You believe that
all your goin' to have
is wretched,
don't think it's worth it
to tell Obertrols from acid.

Sieged by this tiny little marble
you let me take the ones
that tasted secret
five, six or eleven—
here's your fun.

I go under like a wonderful third time,
pretend like I'm someone else.

I don't look very good today,
was sieged by
carbolic upset last night,
the melt of a minute
replenished with a
sudden swallow.

That's all right.
You'll go, very pure, and
I'll sneak out with yesterday,
my mouth sexual with
scenes I don't understand.

Didn't want these scenes

I can't get interested enough
to be up by eleven,
to have to pretend I
meet the requirements to
get ahead.

I don't think it's worth it,
to be other than what I am so I
take all these Obertrols.
I was up all night,
dazzled by my madness.
Wouldn't mind going
to the hospital this afternoon—
no, I'm not courageous enough.

What's going to happen to me
when I start to want this?
You know I really feel the
scream of blame is law.
I couldn't score in the bathroom
and it wasn't enough to call.
I figured that you didn't want these scenes
over and over again.

I would like to be gone

I'm scared of what I'm
starting to find:
lists, like that one,
of heartbreaking news
written as romance.

Night Time can sometimes be
very evil.
Have you thought that
she believes in what she's doing,
has spoken of
shocked reaction,
the world she found reading water.
She doesn't like to go anywhere,
just hem someone into
next Tuesday.

I would like to be gone already
because I believe her.
I lost so many things last night
at the factory.
It's safer not to return.

Slippery noise

It’s not good for you
to unleash ruins,
one by one
along the rough.

I kept hearing them drop,
slippery noise in the throat.
No rest, just
a little bit dead.

For twelve hours I wanted a
witch’s heart, the strength of one artist,
peaked to heaven on dexadrine.

When it finished I
got scared you
wanted to leave.

Just tell me to sleep, to
lock up whatever
I can take care of and go.

I should go.

Truly tacky

There's nothing to hold onto with
honesty but Jack Daniels and
Denny can't afford it.

There's an awfully high price
to sarcasm,
the breaking of his
most famous thing.

He came before my opinion,
divine in a different way.
He called Bob Dylan the
father of art,
considered painting unpleasant,
a little bit like trying to
surprise his soul.

He's the number ten artist.
You might have seen his work:
pop, awake.
He's trying to get bohemian,
get some change for the bus.
Truly tacky.

You see me around

Whenever you see me around it's
with you and Star, the one behind the pole.
Someone said it's tragique, but
I can't afford to bother with
anyone else and
whenever it's just us the sky is
like an old movie.
Star said to come right over to fix.
It's imperative we are delivered.
Let's go.
The lights let you get there.

Louder please

I was the second inside.
Oh Jesus—never seen anybody beautiful.
“Louder please,” she said.
Thoroughly conquered she
took off,
ran down the stairs.
That was the minute I recognized her.
I didn’t know what caused that.

She wouldn’t return.

The Delmonico Hotel

The atmosphere in her is like
an aura of three horses.
She lost a baby
at the Delmonico Hotel.
The minute I saw it,
it looked like something so precious.
Devote a name.

I never know what to say, just
sit at the table.
Please do not disturb.

Oh, when am I going to be sated?

I thought I was a beauty, my look a
golden power.
But those characteristics are
all traders, short of sex.
New York is the goddess I pay homage to
every night but even she is a
misleading instrument,
attracted to all the
young things who do everything
to be the people I admire.

Oh, when am I going to be sated?

I never understand
who they always look to.
I thought I was courageous at sixteen but
can't inhabit the unbelievable.

By the green door

Here we are at the Factory and
there's nobody here, no camera.
We'll just have to wait
by the green door.

I won't jump.
I would like you to run upstairs,
tell them of your problem,
spray apologies at my feet.
I don't want any music,
do what you want with the television,
the gun, virginity.

I hope it doesn't look demented,
throwing heaven down
behind the garage.
Guarded, there's nothing here.
If there's ever been a way, we'll find it.

The Oracle I.

—The oracle is open and I think I have a dime. What's troubling you?

You're going to give me lessons now?

—Tell me what you want to know. I think you should tell, because pretty soon you won't be allowed up there. You won't be one of the fabulous.

It's hard to know how to be good.

—You're obviously off to a late start.

I did want to become perfection for a while, plugged in, one of the group.

—Shall we smoke?

No, this is just all right. I'll tell you about it but would you hold this problem?

—Hell is a hard Sunday. It's gonna be work to be kind, to become anything else.

Have you ever seen anything more?

—xxxxx

The Oracle II.

1.

A friend of mine wanted me to follow him to you.
I suspect it's strange around here.
I have no eye; it's too tight.
Don't try to hypnotize me into deep meditation;
  I just wanted to talk.
We'll pretend it's a strange Saturday with
no one's name in it.

2.

I was up here before you were,
you people who can waste the oracle's time.
Do you realize how busy she is?
The oracle has twenty minutes; it will be closed shortly.
You have no eye and no right to come up here to
  understand now.
Weird looks too small on you, that's how much you know
  about
perfect fit, difficult hours.
Open a wire then get out of Adelphi.
The oracle is reserved.

Like a switch

Did you get the tape?
I've never seen anything that made me look more stunning.
Taught to be terrified he
recovered the reason to call,
said goodbye, screamed a heavy listen.

He just sorta gets that way,
been trained to pick up, want.
Did he ever say what was the matter?
No, never answered.
He might have been closed,
stomped a thought like a switch,
a machine meeting a coat of rings.

I don't want to frighten anybody,
just told him that you'd
probably take it,
keep the money on you like there's
something you can do.

The Oracle III.

—Close your oracle. It's twenty minutes later. I've learned nothing.

—You can't mean that, hovering between a face and a great lesson from today's session. You wanted to know something.

—Close your orafile. You shouldn't let me spend all your life reading coughs. I'll get up.

—Then you'll never know what it is to be eligible for pleasure. Don't you want correspondence to form around your knees?

—I see it now; the streets are just full. I have to be heading up there.

—You don't know the way, really want to say you know it all. Your call came. Why don't you wait?

—I'll see you later.

—If I can ever do anything for you again.

—Close the oracle.

When we're in the streets

Just a kid, you
must be really friendly;
you can't really tell
if there are certain pieces of filth.

I would do it anywhere, even in my
parents' home.
You can't be hard-assed,
as nice as anything else.
I like the experience of
tiny hard lips, asshole cycles with that
special flavor the
guilty wear.

Nothing happens when we're
in the street.
Pucker, that's all anybody does.
If somebody says to you,
"Oh, please sit on my face,"
you've got to acquiesce.

You must have that
certain thing.
I walk out and they
don't do anything.

What had to be done

Brooklyn squat.
I was hysterical
in the middle of the
living room floor.
There was this one guy
who told me he was real and I said,
"Please."
Please get this
shit out of me.
"I'll try," he said,
enormous hesitation in his mouth.
He walked me to somebody's room,
told me about Fire Island,
told me it was
getting warm outside.
I looked up,
a modest process of night.

I know when I have to open up.
One by one, mouthfuls of recall,
twenty minutes of a lifetime.
"I know," he said, and
I showed him what had to be done.

I was in these stories

You can fuck yourself knowing you'd like
arriving after it was over,
wherever I was in these stories,
a push to the bottom when I was
coming back up.
For you this door's closed.
Take the hard-on down and
give me a camera, a hand,
seventh clatter on the other side.

Take what I showed you.

Diet pill poison

Listen: Josephine's a
stem of a girl.
She hasn't even got any
luck, only
diet pill poison,
a measure of games.
She doesn't have it left to love,
a cherry of reason that she's
not giving to you.
You have to learn how to
handle her if you make out.
No, you don't want her.
She's probably onto this,
nervous we'll all judge.
I don't know how far you can go
for the sake of average.
Don't accept scared. It could show.

On the swings

Why don't you do it at the park
on the swings
tie a rope around your head cause
you can't expect to sit like this
at the edge for six months,
eight years,
stretched to the point of ancient,
that face pulled down,
been around.
Study the ejected. Think clinical.
This process goes on every minute of the day.
You've gotta have something to do.
You can't expect to reach forward with
a chain at your back.

Give up

What's wrong with the
girl's mouth that we
can't make her a star,
make her be the new Jesus.
She likes war and likes to
suffer from smart, another spell.
She went down on me
once in the bathroom to
work her way up.
I was so happy but she was
really calm about it, another difference,
no control.
She doesn't want to be fucked,
rotten uterus a
poor start.
We would really have to think that
nothing can stop us.
Is there a taxi to another girl?
I want to give up.

What she loves

I don't know how anybody grows like that,
a drug fiend since she was twelve years old,
pretty face, young muscles.
She told me bits and pieces of her story,
a child leftover frail, parents deadly,
conscience drugged to make
places for your hands to fit.
She indulges herself in disappointments,
frantic for someone to
believe the world owes her.
I couldn't mind her; you just know she would
piss on the favor.
She wants very desperately to be true but
I've seen what she loves, seen what she's
nervous about.
The arrangements she adores got me.
I couldn't move her toward anything better.

Imagine now

My mother, gorgeous on screen,
says she hates herself.
I've heard every little movement,
lies the sound of God raised towards torture.

Perhaps she doesn't quite believe it as much as she says;
I figured that out a long time ago,
resigned to the height of her every dig,
bright to its extremes.

"Please don't come home for Christmas,"
she said, always drags it up to my face,
assured no one else would question her passions,
my father viciously involved.

I'm a product of her and she is that good.

Imagine now that
all mothers should be burned.
Savage rest, no one else involved but family.

In the cellar

She was married before,
sight unseen to
such a motherfucker,
squashed her nose,
upset everything.
He sent her right out, disappointed,
wearing her old contract.
She's taken to fainting in the hallway,
tried to kill herself with a
plastic bag in the cellar.

They took her away to the hospital
for being bruised and demented.
She can't go to bed alone and I
think she has LSD in her closet.
I can, I recognize the voice but I'm
not sure of anything else.
The nurse wouldn't let her out.
She told you everything will be all right but
I don't know.
I wouldn't be bothered waiting for her.

Race with the pictures

This is a weird day,
twenty-four hours on tape,
a long ways off from tomorrow night.
I had certain things planned,
doctor's visit and
a starring proposition with Ondine.
I think he may be asleep and
so are you right now.
I'm gonna have a little bit of difficulty
being filmed with a
coat of insipid thinking.
Look at that ass, wanted.
Race with the pictures. Unwrap the evening.

Your caution

I thank God you're on just
two of these beautiful pills;
I'm on five and
in wonderland,
a combination of my
overindulgence and
your caution.
I gotta get my dress on but
don't know anything right now.

You know what you have to find
for us with your society teeth?
Fifteen milligrams of these obies.
Do you know anybody we could
even ask?

Make them pay for it with a
final compromise.
You'll never get through with
no money but
they should just
want to be around,
come in for an injection.

Why should we be sensible?
I feel fine
day by day with
whatever happens here.

Poke fast I'm
dehydrating,
running just to answer my thinking.
Someday soon you can be in it,
if you want to.

What she did to write

Who told you that
you can really get involved
with her?
I think she's only
ninety-eight pounds of
mental strain. Die of
acute earache.

She got into trouble for
being the second woman to
go up in a blaze,
told it herself on television with
her brother's leg in drag.
Left me cold,
air in my throat thinner.

You were actually pleasant last year.
She's sort of changed you; you're all
hard, no need to eat or reason.
You ever heard what she did to write?
Used lovers, doesn't wanna name
or love very well.

Find a way to get through
to tomorrow, over this.

For keeps

The minute I take amphetamine
I believe the opposite of time and
regular nonsense,
thinking about you beaten,
broke up.

I never thought about anything but sleep;
now I love the taste of revealing
what you taught,
imitating puzzles for 3 1/2 hours.

Can you see what happened?
I couldn't stand what was at stake
after you;
I get hungry and go to the night.

After you've taken a lot it
does this in everyone,
makes me so very sick which is
really too much for anybody to endure.

I used to make sure to eat,
thought this was all for keeps,
supposed to be fun.
Really.

Really.

The perfect face

I overheard his mind,
guilt living up inside,
intelligence shut off but
he's got the perfect face.

We've been feeding him white gloves and
rye bread every morning,
chopped up a list so excited I could
little afford it.

This should be unbearable,
that he refuses to function but
we lost him a long time ago,
found him burned and
just deadly afraid of his mother.
He comes from that kind of family,
tortured and tormented in a
house full of dog shit.

He's completely out of it; crawls in public and
dies every time I call his name.
He sees me for just a
second or two.
I would never go back to find him again.

Just stay

I'm just following you around, all
fucked up on three sentences
I heard the other night.
You wanted to be one of my
lovers at one time; the way you
told it sounded atrocious,
music not played right.
What to do with
the volume of you;
I wanna wear it, fit you
to my statue, a presentable valley.
I like what you gave me in
the back of a warehouse,
made it look like there is
so much we have.
Come here; listen to me. I'm
in your apartment. It's the
only way to do this.
Don't talk. It's not that bad.
Just stay.

Touch me

I’m at the Factory,
just got here.
This is the first time you
haven’t been here.
I’m sorry, baby,
I couldn’t get well
on the side of the street,
couldn’t help but
come apart.
I’ve been calling you
since I arrived;
ran out of a restaurant,
forgot I parked the car
right in front.
Too heavy; there
should have been
someone to keep me up.
Touch me;
come Monday
I’ll be all right.

Sister

Sister fainted out shopping,
wound up a wreck
nervous to get something to eat.
She's so fat but
just drinks vodka,
kept down two cans
right and wrong.
She'll probably crawl in bed,
get off the minute I tell her
I don't think she should have
done all the things
she's been doing.
She's sure it's my fault,
your fault,
doesn't know she
drove us out.
Wait until she's lying down
to leave, get outside of her.

Lucky

I'm all witch,
a secret eater down to my dress,
walk on three quarts of vodka a day.
I just can't stand around here all night,
taking out all my very personal crud,
talking about what all this is.
I'll have the drug for you but
see if you can get off on liquor,
lucky you're nobody I can blow.
You don't wanna take the whole thing;
this mark and all it has made belongs to me.

Severe atmosphere

The obertrols didn't work;
I tried yesterday to speak
but nothing cleared up my voice
like the severe atmosphere
of the morning.

We started off to find Ondine,
drag him to Queens to pick up.
I thought I slept last night but was
just fighting, instituting moron rules
we need for our dear beloved.

Just hold what's allowed;
we have to start right,
full of nothing,
entirely down.

Essential nerve

An essential nerve
gave us the message
to destroy sunshine,
eliminate the sound of rest.
Please, please
I explained it
once before, promised it's
not gonna be for long just
a little bit of a
rough time to get to
where I was going.
I didn't expect you
to really be here, stupid enough
not to leave.
I know when we should
be afraid of an insulting downtown.

I'm sorry; you go back to sleep.
I'm sure this deserves
to get across as
the way to something pretty.
Let me do it. It took me
one and a half hours to wait
for a horrible being.

He told me exactly when to go.

The job we have

I'd love to speak to Gerard but he's
somewhere on Eighth Street,
disgusted with the telephone,
disgusted with people.
He knows I allow you
to take pictures of me, furious I
won't go without you.
I really am a property
being shown to just anybody,
wanted on the edge.
He says you shouldn't be like that,
should at least let me go out but
I don't blame you, don't want to see
what I don't have.

I won't go without you, my dear.
I would never do anything like that to you.

I can leave Gerard a message,
spell out the terrible job we have.

A little poke

I used to dance like love,
can't get back to
what I wanted,
flailed on amphetamine.
Everything's crippled now,
gentle injections designed to steal,
take the skin off the hurt.
Beauty mark a cramp,
sick off a little poke.
I write notes every night in public,
signed to find what I need,
conclusions, if there are any.
I could put my new dress on and
be all right, learn to like
the answer I know I've got.

So phenomenal

I don't want a biography now,
all these things I
don't need to explain.
I'd never be right,
wouldn't get let back in.
I looked so phenomenal
sick, all white.
I owe it to myself to
deny hope from head to toe.

What I can't see

The day-old pictures don't speak of an effort
but talk totem, tell the whole
lazy story of this
world of nothing.
I'm never guilty of a nasty favor but
everybody else is
in the way of trying to teach what
I can't see.
Unfortunately you have to
turn on the light yourself to
demand proof, sheets of the
right picture.
Go ahead, take them
just like this.
I wanna make the place,
show I have been here.

Road blocks and cigarettes

I'm dead, so sick of
being stoned,
voice shaking, can't help it.
I'm so over last week,
that big party you had.
We were all over the floor,
frightened of Gerry sitting
on the toilet,
everybody talking about
a message in the camera.
Did you hear it?
One picture and it was speaking,
something very old in it.
I threatened to shut off the
sounds we hallucinated and
everything we smoked,
road blocks and cigarettes and
death behind the door.
I don't have anything except pot,
wanna moment to try to be myself.

Believe in what we can find

You'll have to excuse me I'm
not enough at all times,
shit, if anything,
didn't eat; didn't know what to let in,
if you have anything to drink.

I don't want to be around anymore,
extracting reality
out of a saucer,
an elegant strangulation.

I lost the light,
not good at being lucky,
destructive circumstances above all
like I promised.
It just stays with you, this
awful answer,
dominant and not yet done.

I think you may be the only one who
didn't go against me for
being so aggressive.
I don't know what you want;
I must have shown,
just for a minute,
the hold that's on me.
I'll stow away and then
you'll go downstairs.
We'll believe in
what we can find.

Just bearable

You're going to hear that I'm
in the raw,
off pot and my
head's gonna choke.
I don't feel that well,
noise in the 4th,
different shifts,
burst so expert.
Do you know it's
really so incredible
to have some talent.
I still have this thing,
just bearable.
I have to stop looking down
for an idea, empty
24 hours a day.
Sorry I can't be polished
in the open.

Lax till eleven

Does Brooklyn call you to stay,
do anything to realize the day?
Don't live anywhere, no friends—
they get boring after a while.
Vary the position,
lax till eleven,
able to go ahead.
Let the city start.

Rosalie

Step on the cusp
forest in orange, raspberry,
you can't see
how much living they call this,
forgetting forward, names in gilt.

Rosalie choked to death on her birthday,
eighteen, and I disappeared almost
everyday, liquid hyphen
tried to hold this year,
wouldn't know how long
age would take.

I feel better now but
don't really care why I
haven't gone out yet,
only have stopping grounds.

You're not gonna watch me
like that.
I tried to talk occasionally but
I only have one avenue,
keep to my old outfit.

Marked

I don't blame the degradation, steel notorieties
sneak out in daylight, broad wonder I
just don't want to lay down.
On the outside stealing
one atmosphere at a time on your toes,
answering to the other,
catch just one dishonor
then it's death, stark space you can pile
over here.
I know what you're marked with,
mixed renewal.
You disapprove of something,
go the way they'll never think of.
Don't apply for what this will entail.

Stick around

Minds aren't made on the fire escape, trying a new
form of blonde,
head mixed up the whole summer.
Don't let him hear what's wrong;
you can learn to say it quick,
voice a chance to
stick around if you'd like to.

All I need

I was English and faking it,
dazzled by the essential tensions
of the city.
I wouldn't live anywhere with no
job in art,
so tired I
just lost it,
a little thing enough for me,
broke wonder.

I don't live that anymore,
sleep in a busted hotel room,
merely all I need.

The pictures

Nerve in quicksand, a
deeper objection to slap trust,
that third word a function of
bad taste.

I don't mind when
people say things like shit,
nothing to do with the moment you
shut my face,
acceptable inconsideration that
does not answer what you can ask.

The pictures become mine,
I realize.
Take off your jacket and
put the camera down;
we owe ourselves a rest.

The young can't rest

You were here once as an old friend,
brought money and the invitation
to move quickly, let go,
let's go somewhere.
12 hours in your car,
you told me to refuse peace;
the young can't rest.
Both of us were handsome,
in a hurry to have
some kind of surprise.

Silk

Don't talk just
hold these voices.
You're fine,
you know.

Don't be sick
about creatures;
the mind is silk and
they are not allowed here.

Outside 8th Street looks
like a risk.
I swear to you
this is exactly
what you want.

Aim the lens

One o'clock I
woke up
down here
on the couch.

No, I never
have a tendency
to become adequate,
turned on so much
to the talking
through a television set,
always disappointing.

Aim the lens at
what you
might lose.

I tried to
kill myself to
correct a lot of problems,
saw a vision
without knowing
to continue with this light,
transfer the
sound of sleep,
push the picture
onto morning.

I should tell you
about last night.

This is how the opera ends

Shoot the fire
put that veil
over her voice, amphetamine dive
up your nose.
Do you know how far
we're getting?
This is how the
opera ends,
finale misprinted
down my leg,
aria the only
true record,
organ of arrangement.
Is that a happy song
she's saving?
She says I
no longer have to listen.

The size of normal

All right, I won't talk
about the last time I saw her,
topless, chewing gum,
the trouble to save her
too much wear and
tear on the heart.
She won't stop this
stolen opera,
wants something else but
it's too ugly,
the size of normal.

I know why she couldn't be clean
but it's not
for you to see.

Prime

The horse is waiting for me, red hair and
green velvet rhythms,
her language shocking.

I'd be so devoted in
satin escape,
Medea in a madhouse
talking abstract with
one tit out.

Music in my mind
badly ethereal,
hope for prime.
No rivals
sing the same parts as me.

Country of women

I heard hideous speak in
the country of women,
red care to the mouth,
mine removed, not sure of
my name, the way out.
I was young, starting all over,
tending to experience,
acute problems.

Queen of rats

I saw Lucretia on the other side of gorgeous,
a Queen of rats who
makes love to sleeping men.
She can't answer the phone anymore,
cut her son for singing and
sees hell on the television,
don't care to pay the rent.
I would have thought her to be good;
don't really care for her anymore.

The hardest things

It's a prolific injustice,
this underrated version of pretty.
Some people can live through the
hardest things but
I can't do it,
can't get over poor melodies.
The only experience we can be heard in
values the most impossible question,
doesn't prove anything.
I'll just lay on the floor
and you could put on the miracle
a little louder.

Atrocity

I know you are
eating God, talk just like an
atrocity,
one rhythm
to your heart—I can't stand it,
a wicked fainting.
Don't make my dress wet
overpowering a silver spoon
bent right in my mouth,
charming one line
up a leg.
Deserve to beat up
a statement as gorgeous as
the mind;
I never heard anything,
just shook.

Different in every color

Y'know I haven't even
seen the ocean,
too busy with this in my hand,
journal that should be a cemetery,
composer of something to
stay away from.
Shut me up;
I like to hear you talk,
hear how the voice is
different in every color,
other sounds stealing thought.
Unpack the one that's
called sensitive.
I will follow as much as I can.

Enough to imagine

Let's not go on about most people,
leave it I do well being a
vulgar pig, tripping over the world,
a combination of Los Angeles and La Warhol.
Wretched imitation I can
only exist on this side of drinking,
running around saying
everything is so beautiful,
a shrill hook left to rest.
I can take hours to confuse,
eight more enough to imagine.

What I want

Don't tell that story 'cause we
all have to be pushed to feed,
a little amphetamine and bang,
six hours of madness and a
lifetime of regret.
Close up I'm not ready,
don't want to rise with a
substitute for a heart,
caught a nasty drug and
took the whole thing.
You're suggesting something very easy;
I could make this what I want.
Just wait right here—
we can have anything.

Portrait of fog

Don't move I'm
listening to the record,
a portrait of fog I
never thought I
could be part of.

Hang around the back and
tell Taxi that everything
is all right.
I smoked the world just,
just,
just,
just to know
what's going on:

white owls,
the World's Fair,
the best hour to
put your name on.

Quiet.

I haven't thought about it much,
have to decide
if I want to.

Been buried

I haven't seen you in a long time,
been buried in the
last line of Ondine's
offensive journal
spilled over
into everything.

My art, a design to speak,
is in the back room,
something to be rid of.
Help yourself. It's just
my life.

A shell of wonder

How much power does it take to get a
group of lions in my arm?
I'll do it myself,
administer the drug,
doctor the whole thing
up your nose,
in your drink—wherever you want it,
I'm fixing what is broken.
This is called getting rid of the present,
fuck it up and we'll
run around,
scrape together a
shell of wonder.

2 days

I asked for
2 days
out of the light,
a special hell of
missing honey,
no leaving
without a snuff show.
I called out, please please—
put it loud,
a break in the gold,
no right
to be around.

Gemini space

Nothing's here just
hallucinations of a
beautiful boy,
remains in
white leather and
Gemini space.

Maybe I'm having
2 conversations at once,
obnoxious compartments
of rush,
an easy inch
of his name.
I should have just
walked out,
not bother with the event
of a thrilling capsule.

In minutes that'll be the end

The way you always
react to the push
signaled the killing.
The one that got us was
just a sigh,
impossible to hear.

We fell into eternal noise,
are now just ruined,
armed to
get rid of that
beautiful picture.

In minutes that'll be the end;
please, really.
We're doing the right thing and
this is going to be so light.

The door is a knife

Get yourself a glass.
I'm going to this other side to
swallow pregnant fire,
escape this act of
strange names.
I would die hurt,
everyone closed off after
this road.
Who was it that asked me—
no.
The door is a knife and
you can certainly stab a
situation.
Leave.
I look cleaner after I've
hit a change.

What I believe is broken

We can't really talk about what happened to me today,
mind devastated ever since.
I was born dirty,
made mistakes but
I want more,
don't have that much to live on.
As long as you're here I'll
play you the album,
wide open it will calm what
I believe is broken.

Turn on the light

Gerard you
better help us
turn on the light.

Be prepared to crawl.
I can't see the cocaine,
it just disappears
up anything I
want it to.

Put some in the
cough medicine
and Coca Cola;
we can start working
to excuse what vanishes.

More than you'll ever see

Gentle things join me
out of the cinder,
singing minds
more than you'll ever see on
me and my time.
I like to feel my
cocaine habit
is giving us nice presents,
a big heart and a
12 hour novel,
moans to music to
start home.

The price of your company

I'll have to think about
the price of
your company
the other day,
a coarseness
for the cameras,
cut love to honor
what you want.

Another show

I can't go to bed with anyone just
bears, skeletons,
put my mask on and
open up.

This is your life,
a stabbed picture
emblazoned with
a hand that fits hate.

This is where I would
walk out in the audience
but my leg's a rag,
nervous to remember
another show.

Bulls

It was the most glorious experience of my life:
pissed on in the bathtub,
small water in protest of
nicer girls.
I tried to ride indelible bulls
to pay for the next day.
I've never minded to get near them,
to get along.
Oh, you can do so many things
with a magic marker.

Certainly monotony

Take care of yourself:
this fuckin trip is
certainly monotony and I
don't have enough amphetamine
to take to New Jersey.
Tin foil anxious it's
horse we need,
contrary condition I've
never seen you at a loss.

In this opera

He said, "y'know baby,"
and I fell right into
the trap,
shot him up a dime bag and
got burned for 30 dollars,
robbbed of shit and laughter.

You would have whatever you wanted
in this opera, stolen radio and a
question I have to hide.

I told him I don't like him but
don't want him to die.
His skin will kill him,
a uranium fool.

Tease the machine

He leaves me and
I'm frantic waiting for
7 or 8 hours in a
tomb of shit,
the price to
tease the machine.

Just cut the character out of me
to kill the hope.
I want to make pretty, but he's
strangling the design,
trying to take it all out of me.

Once in Brooklyn

I'm just trying to
have a lot of fun in
New York City but I'm
very tired and I'm
not gonna do it
in the bathroom again.

Once in Brooklyn I
engaged the noose.
What a relief to hang here.
Turn out the light;
I don't see the point in
conversation.

One night only

hey look:
take my dress quickly.
i like the idea of
knees down,
one night only,
the real way
to the fire.

Little yellow things

Do you have any grass?
I know it's going to ruin me but
what can I do?
Swallow those little yellow things and oh shit
I have phenomenal hysterics.

I can't clap my hands to that.

Play calmly

We have to be nice and quiet about
that stuff I gave you. Play calmly it's a
raving mind, get you sick for a
day and a half.

Do you know how terrible it was that I
couldn't give you the ocean?

It's an opportunity for contact, time you
shouldn't have.

I'm always around.

What life

My voice has changed completely,
undone in his basement, getting rocked.
Amphetamine kept me up all nite.
I just have to get dressed,
smoke pot to come around.

What life.

Why don't you blow my brains out.
I don't want to do it by myself.

We all have our failings.

Trouble ahead

I haven't been in the river
to wash another story,
my feet drunk
on a tight phrase.
You're not allowed
to make a call
beyond the forest;
I think of you in wood,
a filthy eye.
I heard your voice,
a promise on the shoulders.
Trouble ahead, it's hard
how you say it.
I won't easily lose
what you can do.

Later tonight

I'm so sick of
that fucking drug,
noise of children.
Do you know
what it took to
get out of here
in the morning?
A dying girl and a
tin foil mind—her name
wasn't Diane.
I'm sure what time
we're going to feel
all right.
I'll probably be
too out of it to
come off.

Tell us if he opened up

Honey,
tell us about the things
that happened
with that ratty mouth.

He wasn't bad,
kept looking at me
like this, exhausted.
It was difficult to
keep up a conversation
with no more cigarettes.

Tell us if he
opened up.

Just a little bit.
First he was hysterical,
dragged in.

He came half an hour late.

Expression alone

She was 28 and
had her own
sick ideas about
sizing you up, not knowing
how to communicate but
interested in the process.
She looked awful, as though she
never listened to
what is young,
expression alone,
hangups in charge.
After about 10 minutes
she left, looked as though
she was having a
rough time.

Smith

I got a feeling of the same streetness on the east side
scratching my point of view.
The place is so dirty I would
spend the night there doing a
guy named Smith.
He said a lot of things that
weren't funny but I was reacting, coy.
He couldn't find a way to say he liked it and I
couldn't get out of the room.

Just summer

You said it's just summer. We were
all playing ourselves, weak,
about to die.
I didn't really say anything
about why I thought we
knew what we meant.
I might have said
three quarters of one instant,
after she said she was a witch.
So far into it now I
can't bear being this dirty,
golden boy games so confusing,
the worst of what we are.

New kind of girl

Leave the door open.
I want to be saved
in my room,
the new kind of girl,
original piece of nothing.
Rock and roll smells like wine;
we can do all kinds of wonderful
with this record on—heavy breathing,
tormented blushes.
Aren't we special; I've never
seen such heaven afraid
of being alone.

I don't care anymore what happens

I'm starved for a nice day,
can't go on with these imitations
rusty mirror EXPOSED—I hate
to be like that.
Talk louder, these are prayers;
mumbling scares
the shit out of me when
faced with myself.
Thank god I have something
substantial to hold on to—a
razor, a smart brushstroke.
I enjoyed every vicious line,
don't care anymore
what happens to me.

What I wanted

We got to the factory to find
a holy thing,
float around like Allen Ginsberg,
veins electric.
You won't mind if I'm talking
very low. STIMULATING is
more or less what I go through
every day, bathe in rags and
terrifying water,
drink all the soap—it makes
the sound softer on
days like this.
It's really not bad at all, you know.
I'm gonna go to India for
peace and contentment when I
have enough of what I wanted.

Grasp the light

At the end of it they
put me away,
taking off seven years for
acting complete, conned and
what else exists?
They grasp the light,
will never speak, a
perverted technique to
take it all down.
I wanna be triple fast and
whenever you say fantastic
realize that you meant it
but I am the sicker one,
the one nobody knows.

Hair on fire

I was the only one with
hair on fire,
leave a light burning,
rattle in the window and one girl
said to me,
"why did you leave with that boy?"
I know there was something about him,
briar patch disguise for sadistic sorrow,
one line I wanted
nothing but fun,
never tried to set him down,
touch weakness.
Bent, he saw what I had.

So easy

It's so easy it
seems like it's endless to
ruin the most interesting things.
I got the bad routine and it
didn't even cut, hurt only
cause somebody told me to
remember I had died,
dirty ivory and sharp stubble.
I left little red envelopes
in the apartment,
bathing suits tied to chairs,
sighs of relief and music.
OPEN THE DOOR.
My brain is SNAPping.
Will I ever be free?
I wish we could open the window.

Young thing

I once knew somebody who said you
just have to reflect torment
and hate.
He wounded every little spot,
driven to burning cold.
But I feel like a young thing
posed in the bath with
you in the room.
Do you realize for one second
there's no other brush stroke?
Thank god I have perfect legs.

Outside brilliant gold

I haven't been home in two weeks,
live on dirty water and
mucous worn sideways.
It's heaven, it's so vile.

I was exasperated and
the cord snapped. I have
all the money you want but
rob like you can't imagine.
I never know the difference
from sublime; my inside is black,
outside brilliant gold.
It's the only way to
wear my words, my mind.

Open up. I need a quick dose.
You can leave any time you'd like to
once I get what I want.

It takes some time

Touch my forehead and
lose your balance. It
takes some time to
get settled.
Garish bruise and
gorgeous swelling,
the tone of your voice was
so perfect I
couldn't lift my head
off the pillow.
I didn't know what to do,
my hands going
to my mouth, high.
The way you reacted
really touched me,
comb my hair
with your fingers,
voices low,
talking around
what I resented.

Bad solution

Ten years I've been related
to a bad solution, take a pill and
give some, too.
I couldn't bear him, a
thirty something psychiatry lesson.
He tried to hypnotize me—
"stop talking"—a half stutter
across the street.
I was a bit bored
with his kiss,
nothing exciting about ruin.

Nite Life

I had such a good time
in your bathroom
on Nite Life Monday,
all witch and
wearing hand-me-downs,
sprays of magic.
Muffled talking was a
history of wit,
one sentence in there a
bad scene, slit wrists and
four minutes that
didn't fit anywhere.
Don't ever play this but
I wish you would kill me.
I just wanna settle here.

In the throat

Let's go out.
I'll find you a pill
to get stuck in the throat,
two then twenty more,
situation breathless.
I won't speak to you,
just nod, block up the sound of
banging noise coming in
on camera.
I don't just want to be a
five minute film.
Hold this. I'll get us a drink.

Sugar on top

I have this trick of things,
music slow,
sugar on top,
spill of Beach Boys—it's
supposed to be like yesterday,
drunk and sorry.

I can't go on.

Leave it all alone

He met me early in the morning
between 8th and Broadway
and he said, “come with me,”
up to his apartment,
two boys sitting around
playing with the Moon. Nobody sang; I got a
headache immediately, said
“I’ll have to go,”
leave it all alone.
They sat there,
asked me to explain it, a
moral security.
I held the emphasis on run.

You've been so kind

Do you know what she got away with?
Anything worth confiscating is
hiding in her closet: blood pressure,
a doctor's coat, 3000 libriums,
a whole population.
She went down the hall and
stole it all saying thank you
for the drugs; you've been
so kind.
I left a thousand dollars
on the bus, didn't want to
say anything.
Everything is weird and
she never saves me.

Between the two headlights

I was transgressing between
the two headlights
T.V. set on the channel
I thought was
my mother, turned away, out of order.
My God
I didn't know
what it involved, to be in
the middle of antagonism.

Hello gypsy

I thought I lost you
the first time you ever
disappeared on the couch,
hello gypsy
spilling drink, taken with
what you can't see,
don't care about anything.
Let me take you out
this weekend, shouting red hair.
A moment won't straighten
your light.

Definite reasons

Look, here they come.
Let's do it again; I'll start
up there, staring at Mercury,
the only sound drowned out
by traffic.
You see something
that I don't;
it looks better on television,
definite reasons
giving to cutting mynas.

I almost fell.

What you just said is
no longer as
much a joke.

Don't come unless you call

I saw some pictures of her in Vogue,
big sheets of paper,
instructions about being used
to perfection—
don't come unless you call or
unless you're beautiful or
unless you know it.

I can see ________ in her,
bad in person.
She started to look groped,
dreary.
I couldn't stand
to write about her.

Those people

You didn't bring me music,
never listen, stall just to
gather blank minutes. Remember those people
we said we'd be? I wanted to write,
be in pictures.

We're supposed to mean something.

The Middle

I'm probably wasting my whole life
trying to understand the
ability to take care of myself.
I'm too tired to bring presence
to one direction, smoke $100
trying to get in the middle
of miserable.
There's only one person
I'm gonna be with and that's you.
Don't be responsible.
I just want this to work.

Stay lost

You keep hanging on
without revealing the habit,
insisting they wouldn't know.
There's got to be a war on
entry to what you knew you forgot;
let it take care of itself.
You're so young to have a reputation.
Be patient and resigned to stay lost.
We must die exactly.

Everything's fine

What you chose to do
is the most true, denying time and
giving up what needs to be done
if I'm to do anything rewarding.
Anybody else could believe in
nice things but I doubt all the time
that everything's fine, attuned to the
strangest step. I'm just the
opposite of you, correspond to
idleness, and that is acceptance when
I die to begin again,
each time a little harder
to have you there.

The only way to live

Leave me alone.
You know you've won
because you're still
a whole incarnation,
one total dimension beyond
somebody like me, sort of half
dragging the thoughts they've
put in your mind, a siege of
routines under surveillance.
It's the only way to live
and yet I'm sitting there screaming,
it's so painful.
I can't forget the habits they've given you.
It's best the submission is over.
Even if I don't matter, they will
and I just can't be rewarded.

Wherever we end

Drunk for three hours
to deal with what is obvious,
dreaming up the same thing—oh I
can't believe we
live in the present.
I discovered I'm out of money and
I'm the same and
I'm struggling.
We're being overheard, lover.
Let me stay. Commit to wherever
we end.

Pig

He knew the realm of
degradation stuck to his
role as pig.
What a fuck, clearly.
True condemnation
is a roll in the dirt,
animal inferno.

Wish

Drawing hell or New York
we made a game of it,
arrested pleasure
rating the depth of my life.
It's just such a struggle
for divinity and stars,
fox raiding a crescent moon,
century a sly diagram
expressing a wish I've
never heard before.

Games

Ondine has games that
no one understands and I
can't see through all this.
I'm missing the moon,
divinity a blot of ink.
Of course the only way to
catch your world of mythology
is to get closer to mockery.

The next word

We have to make a symbol
with mixed voices,
all the world in
one night too obvious
for the next word.
You've got the head of a
buffalo and I've got
the fourth noise,
round laughter too much
to be all right.

Name of the game

I never heard the real name
of the game we played.
Near to non-being we're
all set to be put together,
to be whole.

What are you thinking
saying God save us all?

The rapid ones

We are the rapid ones,
going down to
get to the unspiritual state.
Damned but indifferent,
earthly ghosts too complicated to
obey. Haunt character, I owe
something to somebody,
nothing more than a
solstice, manner come back
when we say spirits.

Worse than the next

Like shit you
come back to haunt people,
just not quite right they
obey a vacuum,
defy they exist.
You're in a negative way
to deny the situation,
say the truth, worse than
the next.
Spit.
Make something right.

One word

Split the image:
you can't have it all,
a bottle of Schlitz and a
combination of crap,
one word and
half a need.
Draw a star, sell it
just that way, like saying
we don't need this,
we have the means.

Blind corner

Put down a
valid word.
I got lessons from
Allen Ginsberg
divided in spit,
thinking eyes in a
blind corner.
Distinguish directions,
three rings and a
sign you can't see.
Not fair, to draw
the opposite God,
looking to fill in
the way.

Even better

We've given now to the ocean,
a dimension of importance
mixed to the point of scary.
Majority sigh
doesn't belong to the others.
We'll get it right,
give it even better.

That middle section

It's gonna be so hard
to pass the power to
another, hell a million times,
that could be
another category.
I keep getting hung up on
that middle section,
detailed insects,
something about divinity
and cockroaches.
I should get through that,
start to see now.

Just for us

Constantly paranoid
this kind of change
isn't so fantastic, but
what could we do
for that one touch,
because this
is just for us.
Shape the words, my dear,
muffled more than that.
Shape what we can give,
a symbol they'll never know.

Hell going

Break the lens.
It's too much to
see these things
coming up at you
stained with
the worst.
I wouldn't have to get
one step further
to go down hard,
hell going to
get to gorgeous.

TV Spirit

A spirit from the TV
lemme see different,
glass category the
evil essence immovable.
I don't know
what you're doing, not ill
but not that spell.
Nobody ever says anything.

Vapors

Start asking what I am,
aim on the bottom
of it all.
I've given exactly
what I can, vapors and a
beautiful angle.
Tell me what I could be.

The Rules

I started the spirit unknown,
G-H-A-S-T what I meant,
the shape too complicated,
turned repulsive but
how can you escape
all the dragging things,
RULES FOR THE FACTORY
OH, HERE YOU GO, NOW YOU'VE
GOT IT,
simple pollution of the idea,
draw mysterious,
have nothing.

Blood orange

A year ago at the factory
I drew just half of a face,
blood was orange,
mouth a curl,
head an eye so hideous,
I think.
It scared me so much
I went up on the roof,
had to tear up something
so sinister.

Poetess

Bang bang,
She kept falling on her words,
saying, "look at those bruises."
They wouldn't understand
a treasure like her,
know you can't go under
to give her a place to stay,
nothing lower if you can't
be the best.

Saint

In a Cadillac I was
patron saint for the blind
that day you were taken
to the hospital,
case history for the masses.
On the ground, glass;
you were stumbling open.
I was just seeing a movie,
short blonde hair while
you transported,
patient and forgotten.

Lipstick

The singing falling out of
my mouth is a seed
to break the window,
one ounce through the neck,
honey denied.
Been on LSD for a week,
walking on the balcony
of the wrong room.
Write three names in lipstick
on the wall so I know
what to aim for.
I'm a little stoned and
can't stand but we
better go where we're wanted.

Thanks for everything

I just have to look at myself
in this shit;
you can crawl into with me
if you'd like to and
place what you can't find
right here, under my life.
Say what doesn't fit;
I have paid for everything and
you're so pretty I
keep thinking I don't know
how to treat you but
we always go for more.

Cherry Lane

Hold this just a moment:
you've stumbled.

Now how do you expect
to be open,
close to time and
have the right to
go ahead?

I'd like you to see.
Go. Run.

Push to tell

Kill me
in a fake voice,
disguising the real day.
Make them believe
we're stars,
unbearable to live with.
They hate me
for being what I am and
all your friends
get so mad at you.
Why should we wait here
like this, with doubt;
come and talk to me,
push to tell
how we are.

Hands off

I was doing your day
but it turned into my end,
putting energy into nothing.
You sit there and say
all my friends have left me,
wiser than us; together, we
make another problem.
I wouldn't endure it but
you're getting to be all I am.

Bridge

I nearly fell across Friday;
it isn't a good day to see.
We should always be moving;
I can't remember to walk out
of heavy days.
You can't leave;
I just get lost otherwise.

You have a way

I'm so casual
standing on corners
transfixed by the undertone
of a grand entry.
Just pick me up,
carry me hypnotized.
You have a way of
being good, of talking
about home.

Darling, it's a curse

Didn't you ever see her,
a faithful reproduction of a promise.
She always dances the moon,
doesn't have to participate in life,
holds this to all of us.

Throw a match only to me
when you run out of all you have.

Something's the matter with time,
her curse passive, slaughtered.

Skipping my head

Walk away. I can't stop
this routine, habit eight times a day,
my head just an explosion all the time.
In the pockets of your coat, hysterics;
I used to bathe in empty techniques,
pissed out a trance, burst out laughing.

Look at us; I'm just above water,
never able to enjoy a day.
You should feel embarrassment,
know to imagine all life.

The night crew

Here we are again, nineteen tapes to fill and
we wanna shop at the liquor store,
ripping dirty black seams until you can get us
some things, blow and tea bags—sell the car.
I'd like to go home and see mom,
take the same street I've given up,
want to cover what we will always be
though I can't see where to go to get there.

Current attack

I don't have a
nice way of hating people,
ripped the vaguest idea,
general plan of attack refused
to argue with you, witless.
Inevitable misery you
insulted me, said I should be
where they can tear me big enough
to get put out.

Just an excuse

Tasteless, I want you,
endurance test
just an excuse.
I don't really consider
that you can
get rid of me,
like God in comparison
to find a way.
I broke a tooth
with the force of fault,
screamed a swamp of
remark, gone but
it's hard
to leave completely.

In the bathroom

Drunk after thirty seconds
I've never been so
hard to believe.
Despicable voice, y'know how
noises keep talking.
All my life I fight,
worse off again.

Expect to fall

I was never so disappointed
coming down,
scream equivalent,
hurt evaluation.
If you say one more thing
I'll throw sand.
Expect to fall,
filthy flow you're
not allowed in the apartment
because you might get
rather pleasant and I
don't understand that.

Hang off the sides

Judas bell
I promised
I would never
walk up this street
again, disguise laughs,
just hang
off the sides
of a veil.
Let me get hold of
suspicions; I don't like
the shape you hit,
sniper lips they'll never
put away what you
tried to kill.
Am I out of it,
am I out of it?
I hope anybody would know.

Throwing tomorrow

Choking the lake
we used to get stoned
on LSD, seizures of sleep
in the park
the only thing
you did so smartly.
Broken opening we
hallucinated everything, throwing tomorrow
out the window,
a bloody heel piercing
the side of what you said.
Arms lithe, night thin
we don't know now
what to say or do.

Neon

She buttoned
the top of her
cardigan sweater,
the original confusion,
said it's unbearable
to dance for everybody,
spirit a neon light.
700 bucks and a
ride to New Jersey,
coming early:
call if you need me.

Baby, go to sleep

I walked her up the stairs:

"Let's not stand and talk here;
I don't feel great and
it's time to say goodnight."

I said to her to try
not to take a pill,
doesn't need them any more,
identity tired, a mountain
all her own, lying up there

on the telephone.

"Baby, go to sleep, snap out,
television a lucky strike."

Can't you see it
all depends
on her to lose.

Oh trouble

She's just nightmares,
can make accidents so easily,
fracturing herself with eye-teeth,
shivers of overdose,
a deep sleep that's
good enough to
ask the same question.

Is this right?

I've never been through it
just watch her,
wait until she
has to give up,
my fault she can't.

After 9

Put the bag down.
The cops are gonna come by
and there's no place
to have it backwards.
Mother of us all,
would you give me a light?
I have the number
in my pocket to get off
but lost it, fallen heavy. There's no place to go.
Who do I look for after?

Stay stuck

Rustling capillaries
so pathetic
stuck some place,
lack of wonder.
Is there any way
I can get to tomorrow
hemorrhaging appendages?
Solid pause.
I should stay.

Like leather

I'm not scared but I
just don't want you
to go through it—
I know who she is,
pretty face,
rundown, raw legs.
You feel all right but
you'll never get out
of her mind unless
you're ten years tough,
dying to live.

The grocery

It's tough
when it's raw
for a year,
out of bread
until tomorrow
but we got
such attention,
just enough
to be taken
to fantastic places.
Let me ask you
what I really wanta:
do you feel
all right?
Because you're
not gonna stay there
all night,
next to the grocery.
I don't know
how we are
gonna get well but
I want to.

No time

The morning you
thought I was ruined
you said to be at
your house in an hour.
By the time I got there
you ran away,
left a cigarette and
I made a mess.

okay baby, I'm afraid.

Don't mention it

I went to Frank
the other day,
broke and everything,
and he gave me some money,
told me to have some drinks:
don't mention it, darling.
I know that by heart,
drunk on the streets
in this yellow light.

Just for nothing

Came down to
buy cigarettes,
two in the morning.
Around the corner
the world is freaky
in hysterics,
holding scared.
Let me go up
to see my friend,
make a phone call.
You don't want me to know
this complete insensibility.

Roxy

Rise: I've been down
and up and I don't know
beautiful things, just
exquisite desert.
Silver film I
didn't see colors,
a class of noise as
big as Greenwich Village.

Is there more?

The look

He took me to this hotel,
said, "I can't stand anybody."
Hostility decided.
A dab of white color
along his nose,
I didn't know he was
getting high.
He laid down on the bed,
a little tired,
remained immobile,
fingers stiff.

I had to get out of the room,
went down to Washington Park,
beyond unbelievable.

That other place

It was the end of
the world so I said,
"I'll lay on the couch,"
couldn't pretend I was
anywhere else.

In my head, the forest,
not listening to the strain,
unkind.

After a while
I realized that I
don't mind dying.

One year

I used to walk into a bar and
scare the whole damn world,
couldn't make out or
name laughter.
I heard from a total stranger
I'm a pile of garbage,
broadcast summer:
I hope you die.

Just wait'll they see our faces, darling.

The backyard

Falling off
the side of your chair,
I'd love to forget myself,
white wine and ginger ale
in the backyard.
I tried to get up,
couldn't make it,
filthy hit.
I never showed you
that I tried.

Sideswipe

The sequence of screaming
banged down the door,
"I must come in to see you,"
get off in the middle of the floor,
old cat got everything but you.
I didn't see that I can't live
without a scene,
you some cute thing,
me, a tigress, muffled.

Music in background

Here. Hold now
I'll get this slap
in the face, secretly.
They don't know
we can dance sitting down,
Supremes in background:
supreme in your position,
the most difficult of all.
Voice fades out,
the second side nobody answered.
All we need is a
black coffee christening,
cold drinks and a scribble
of insult right in front
to remind you we should leave.

Have a little more

Sick on a pill
you'll die all day,
nothing to eat and
not very hungry.
Put this record on,
cluster around the
unbearable and
I will take care of this,
the only way you're
gonna get around it.

Found

The back of a book said
to connect the dots
from the side of feeling,
so messy now, admiring
muffled categories,
this thing called the middle.
Trying to find out what symbols
go where is enough
to pull on anyone. I thought better of it.

The ratings

I didn't like the girl in Brooklyn,
looked like dread applied to nothing,
quality under a rating.
She even smiled disconnected lines
when we said we're through with her.
What game is this,
one to ten I've gotta give names
and symbols to these people.

It even hurts

Vile abbreviation enough,
Rolling Stones in background
singing something about
how it is, the girl
who calls six times a day—
you want more, deserve a
fair chorus.

Must we be

I've got to put
Saturday afternoon down,
three keys, one for the conclusion
we'll never come to,
much better than me.
Party falls, bent to
forget this game.

Question more than that.

In the background

Painful autographs and the
company of dull music:
step up and get it,
I'm not unfriendly,
just very special.
Someone in the background says
you can have it, boy.
I can't quite take your hand,
nothing on yesterday,
nothing you wanted to see.

Bodies

At that party
at the factory
I saw you smoking
something strange,
took time to lay
small creatures
on the terrace,
alive with noise.

Out of our minds
we went to the toilet,
bodies imitating
something beautiful.

Dancing in a line,
I was asking to see
that picture we took,
the three of us, enormous,
what we wanted.

That other friend

What makes the person?
Faded good looks
dig at this face,
edge of a valentine.
He really changed a lot,
teeth don't help,
compel the image
of a hustler
living red, wrong.

It doesn't matter.
I still think he's beautiful.

His name is Jodie

Thin boy in the black sweater,
what a face. I'll bring him
up to the factory,
overlook the hustler.

I know the words to
"Satisfaction" but I
haven't climaxed in three and a half years.

You must know
that you're beautiful,
sixteen year old standing up there,
god in the mirror.
I looked like you,
cracked a headache
through the years.

Oh, the things you do
to yourself.
There's nothing left
to admit.

Central Park Lake

It always goes on
in a certain part of the park,
the right vibration
between the rocks
every other second
in springtime.

Morning, an envelope
with a little note
saying I'm only kidding
about you, too nice
to do like that.

Complete picture

One more pill is like a
near step to death,
head on a subway track,
brainless and beautiful.
Blood, complete picture
blackened out.

Operation severed,
this is almost a shock,
aged seven years
in a minute.

One is enough for me.

The first city

Blown out it's
obvious I'm dying,
told her I was a genius and
sat up all night
burning holes in my house.
She kept waking me up,
asking me how to do it.

People will talk.

--

On the dance floor I
claimed the last hunting place,
sculpting city mentalities,
my time outdated,
moved to the obvious.

I've been taught it's
all you need to say.

--

Spent, I'm going to write
everybody's age,
push right on to
what we used to be.

We could have that again.

Velvet

I only saw her once
on the street,
mid-winter bones
hanging from her fingers.
I could feel her
down to the curb,
bold side born up with
this idea you can't learn.
She ran, green skirts
all the way
to the ground.
Cold, I couldn't figure her out,
brilliantly in love.

Mare

I met her at
a house on 7th Street,
convinced her she was gorgeous,
claimed her as a child.
She injected everyone
with rat poison;
we all lived.

She tried to escape once,
dove out of a window,
walks around like
she don't remember.

Satin ribbon and broken glass

It was the day that
the trees were planted on 7th Street.
She took all those sleeping pills,
dreamed that she heard conversations
with a cat with one eye out,
fed an altar but never
fed herself.
Satin ribbon and broken glass,
she had a page of hallucinations
like nobody I've ever known,
a feather of piss hanging off of her
she'd say, "I can't move."
She was trying to die
in her own tomb.
We had all moved upstairs,
200 seconals to chew up,
her own trap to be built.

Old bones

She hadn't spoken to me for two weeks,
called me up filled with pills:

"I'm not dying. I'm just splitting."

This girl goes nowhere.
She's not the type.

I ran over.

"You're so intuitive," she said,
candles flickering like old bones.

A limp cross, I had to keep her awake.

"You fool," she said, laughing.

All I remember

Crawl onto the stretcher,
body swollen.
A letter on toilet paper,
drag of the wrists,
beating fire, island a costume,
so happy just to feel.

This was before

My most unbearable mind
chased out of my somebody else's apartment—
"I'll beat the shit out of you,"
every line injected with Jack Daniels,
so spaced I didn't know if I was dead.
Legs freezing, extremities violent,
head going down I lost my timing,
lost myself—"I've got to go home"—
left my mind on the corner,
calling to get out of here.

She said

In big, green ink she wrote
“you bored me to death,
brought me to break these faces.”

Don’t touch this life;
it’s changed so much.

Trouble

She had no concern for money,
lived in a deserted ruin,
turned on to amphetamine at twelve.
Under her pillow, two loaves of bread.
Up her nose, nothing but foam,
her throat rock hard,
veils of sweat on her face.
What would you do to her?
No purpose, she owes nothing.

The Mercury

Walked down to the basement,
stood there for twenty minutes.
We had a whole bottle,
could have died like that,
afraid to go anywhere,
face carved with perfect poison.
Very tired, dropping from the picture
wasn't anything we thought of.

Am-phet-a-meen

I don't want to
get caught up with
narrating sympathy,
telling the story
hung up in the corner
but I have no money,
shot all these things
with a dirty needle,
had to sit right
over there.

You don't have to dig me out but
would somebody give me a dime, please?
You used to like me.
Who knows you still care? One of these days we'll
come back, really high,
play it all the way.

The clock

She needed a dirty minute
out of the clock to
pick up a pretty boy,
the thinnest star
from a distance
calling to go on,
to run the tough way.
Wait: the strange know each other,
deliver the story of tears.

This piece

Outside these
neon lights
the deep heart of
all things mad.
Let me have it,
notes hung on
skinny legs,
a ticking exhibition
gradually slowing.

Sunshine on our sides

Writing this in the closet
I heard the word,
one more second of happiness,
tripped over my own regret.
Say a few words and
lock the door;
the lights won't answer
because we have sunshine
on our sides.

Not a thing

All I ever did was
let her in, door opened
on a nerve, insulted
her reasons,
attack on everyone.
Under breath, the matter
of opinion,
entitled to more than ever.

Everywhere I go

Down at the end of the city a
lunatic fringe,
that wail of lost life.

I didn't hear her
screaming from the street;
they said she called up,
don't know why she
went out of her way,
out of her mind.

You're the one that drops
these stars
all over the place. I see them
everywhere I go,
deathly ill with delusions,
sicknesses like something
down the drain.

I never saw her that way,
didn't know she had already
made up her mind.

Girl on fire

Her mother said,
"what's that white powder you're sniffing?"
staying awake to take
LSD, banging down the walls.

I remember her face when you said she
coulda been turned back
the other way.
Offended, she put all these voices
into the streets,
set fire to herself.

She really believed
it was very strange out there.

Sleep

Twice at the edge
you threw up the
bottle of vodka,
infected every nerve with
the middle stories.
Let it spread,
put you to sleep.
There's no reason
for you to give
too much.

Seeds

We grew up in the same neighborhood,
spoke to her on the phone just once.
Why not accept friendship?
Something besides force.
All she did was cry; I don't blame her.
Hand around her throat
nearly killed her.

What have you done?
What seeds have you taken?
They seem to be
a large part of me.

Telephone rings

She's got that little girl look
on her face, says
"I give the best shots in town,"
a fiend in the corner.
Music speeds up,
telephone rings and
even I can't tell
she's much better,
sounds like somebody else.
Bag of pot and a
beautiful story,
she hates to be alone,
bearing all this by herself.

Powder

Wrap the matches on your leg,
stretch the burn,
sick on fire.
I'm heavenly blue circle,
nothing but my name
all over the walls now.
I had to swallow the last exit,
crossed the night.

Where does the sound come in?

Her voice, sugary,
plugging it
right into his ear:
come to the inner circle.

You can't be too guarded
when we've been out
all day long.

Everything, everything

Well, I've been drinking,
the same show you
used to think was my strength.
I'm not supposed to go home
to get my clothes till tomorrow
when you've gone through everything—
was anything left?
My stash, the blood:
my dear, I used to agree with you,
too much alike.

I didn't see it was over.

The doctor

I get what I want;
Strangelove, they call me,
save my urine, every pill, for tea,
keep up with the boys who
want another hallucination—
a woman in white, the perfect moan.

Come in, rest. I have more.

Biphetamine

I'm still the same
taking 20 milligram blackbirds,
fatter capsule, longer action.

Name what I do:
white, blue, red,
strength stuck,
round wonder
I'm light,
completely marvelous.

The answer

Tell me your name and
I'll tell you what to take:
it's part of the deal known as the last ring.

I'm what happens
when you decide
to plug in, know the
trip of the pill
just to stay up.
You see, I'm a genius,
now dead, finished with breath.

I know something frantic,
can make you short of time,
heart awake,
permanent palpitation.

Allow me in, give me
a little bit of you.

Prelude

Come on over here tomorrow
and I'll give you poke.
I want to be the pin,
shot of wild pink
completely concentrating on
what puts you up.

Prelude to frantic:
it sounds like a ritual,
a vulgar dig
to the head of the answer.

Maybe you don't know

You weren't open
long enough for me,
whispering 'that was in your head.'

I'm nothing you came for.

The next hell, hyper white,
sensitive to a muscle of pain.

Usual, I gave.

On my mind

Do you remember the studio?
You were writing notes to Ondine.
I was on another trip,
not willing to land.
What did you find when you left?
I don't think I've been there before,
don't go out much, no.
I'll think about it all night,
so much on my mind,
don't admit to one thing.

Sink

Sitting up in bed
I see sky dropping,
whole side of my heart jammed.
There's not much space
for anything in this town,
scene closing in on us,
nothing else to hang up.
Out the window, the other age.
I'll tell you what it is but
we have to go.

Straight in my eyes

Can I come stay
in your apartment,
I went on
another diet,
three quarts of
vodka a day,
had a fight with
my mother,
decided I was
leaving home.
She heard about the
medicines I'd taken,
looked straight
in my eyes,
right here, higher—
don't tell me
that it ruins
anything.
All the pills, y'know,
gonna fuck me up
so good you
wouldn't believe it.
Patient to bed,
I lie there,
think of where
I could be.

Tuinols

Shove my mouth
dangerous,
chasing me with
tuinols, clouds
bleeding the night,
amphetamine mixed
I'm floating, sealed
something I
never told you about,
never touched.

Carry on

Needles sharpened,
boiled sleep,
I have nothing left.

I used to get high,
now carry on dull,
sterilized tradition.

Sorry I had to do it.

Of course

What is this you brought me—
a quart, pot—
did you finish the vodka?
I need more tomorrow.
You know I
have things to do,
don't belong here, of course,
might be
sneaking out soon but
this trip, Smirnoff
and grass, it's more than
I got, more than I want.

Went to pieces

I wanna tell you why
I'm like this,
voice garbled,
stomach in pieces.
I'd die for my liquor,
electric high, sold
ten obetrols the other night
for just a little gin,
sorta never come back
to what I was,
needless, skulled.

Carry it around

Bitter machine
I'm not gonna sit
and shut up, end the morning
the other side of ugly.
Woke on the verge of
being very frantically up,
wouldn't sit in that
god-damned place and
not get high,
fucking purple curtains
and my bottle of vodka.
Gotten worse, passing
the time I can't stand
to do without my bottle.

Something else

The message came out of my mouth
at the same time you were talking—
try to say it, a clue more recent,
something so ugly,
my idea of what I
think we're getting.

Ride a high journey

It's hard for me to tell I love her,
her greatest sensation a trick,
gonna be out there
all night,
some weird
nobody else likes.
Eroded through the ages,
she said,
"can I have a pill
to go to sleep..."
Not the same anymore.
Whether that's fantastic
or awful I don't know.

One other day

I don’t know about
pearls ad white gloves, girl,
heaven a body of
bad love right off Broadway.
See the star, one other day,
production of half a trip.
I never leave, just dig on
what I can get.

In Berlin

He picked me up
in a bar, dancing,
the sound of a story
to the left of center.
Walked out with him,
so sick on the street—
not very me at all—
trying to think of
something normal.
I came out of it
in the morning,
deaf to fabulous,
cast in the end
of the picture.

The great white way

Ultra Violet says she
has a present for me,
a mixed mess in the hip,
gear the answer I ordered,
an important question
without the sound.
High the great white way,
say that it won't kill me.
We're gonna have a
scene tomorrow, darling,
flying on the upper right quarter.

Spending my life

You know what I just got?
A big nebutol, think they can
put me to sleep, just put me
more up there, know me
so well I just wanna
dance around my life,
pushing too far black,
be out in a year, down to
whispers in a month.

Wind-up baby

I've taken a
stark amount of nebutols,
a blue circle sleeping pill and
I thought I was a wind-up baby,
flying out to heaven, lost.
Make me turn the television off.
I'll see you tomorrow,
gonna bring the right craving.

Know the strange

Speak immediately:
I'm not alone in this
conversation, wire eulogy
speared to the wall,
a demand to take care of
the opening to your voice.
Entire wish, all of your room a
night of mine, first time for years.
I've always been told you
know the strange.
Come right over with
all we could have.

I can't speak it right now

Fortune blind I'm
very high, pause for weeks
thinking in Spanish.
It is better if I'm dumb,
losing time, deaf accent
I will keep what you said.

Recovery

Let me come up by myself,
back to your room,
black and blue by
the end of the night—
I don't give a shit,
it'll be done in the morning.
Take me down, fictitious by yourself.
I won't go away
after what I've had to drink,
entirely open, the recovery of
what I have to show for this.

Fading away

Just keep talking,
I will have a
little more vodka,
undercover,
a mixed hell with
you mad at me
because I don't care
what's drinkable.
Throw me out,
I just can't get
used to you,
this room the
hardest thing
about tomorrow.

Trouble in the door

You're gonna laugh when you
meet me, my dear, head off,
hemorrhaging booze,
legs and arms black and blue I'm
one of the few people that will
speak to pokes and pills,
sensible malnutrition that's
all about the raise of a glass.
Losing circulation nothing gets me drunk
like trouble in the door,
capillaries ill and everything a
reason to trip.

Stay here

Let me tell you about costumes,
sliced to forget,
a test on what will change.

I'll stay here with you on the floor and
in the morning we'll have breakfast, coffee,
dressed in a dirty T-shirt and a cocktail, chic.
I'll read you the menu, reserve admissions.

You know what I'm doing.

Distance with the bottom

I carry around your
tender choice,
steer a boneless need
to have everything.
You see I've changed.
You're getting elegant, cold,
blended with the
bottom of the day.

Rotten

Whipped cream and a
lost dress,
rotten fruits she gasped,
pitiful meat,
taste of honey calling.

Witch girl

Coming down,
wanting to talk to you on
Second Avenue I
met a witch girl,
black sheath dress.
She wrapped around me,
scared me for the first time.
Everybody's life here
this side of dirty, oh,
I've seen something else.
She got it right.

Wilder

Drive me to the point of high drag,
complete to strange,
shits and fingernails,
I can take it.
Nobody in the whole fucking world
is wilder than I am.

Entourage

Darling, I never go to bed,
got bored with it years ago,
God, it must be 2:00 now.
I'll call some girls,
polka dot entourage,
seven days around me I'll
take care to know the morning.

Practice

You in the night,
wild static,
practice of blood,
a poke to get off.
I showed you
how to do it,
pretty much
taken away
most of us,
drop of care,
quickly master
the click.

A lot to lose

Oh, here I am again,
the distinction of strange
a little quick for me.
Librium is a lot to lose and
I'm terrified to eat,
body fantastic I
never thought of it before,
tucked away and
taking up the perfect moment.

Young painter

She said we sound alike,
not well, just rough,
turned to shit,
enthusiasm for a lover
ruining me: you thought
we made this work.
Wake me up talking about
marijuana, drinks,
the best place for doing nothing.
Oh, go on,
go on.

I'll divert you

Sunshine ran out of here this evening sick,
said to me, "If I could see you in a while."

"I'll be somewhere else, unless I need some diversion."

Faint, she thought I was
putting her on,
meagre twin to
tell me what to think.

I'll call her when I
get off work.

The echo

Say it again,
I'll be the echo:
this is my life,
less born.
I could never be
the high note.

I'm glad nobody's talking to me.

Interruptions

You can't hear the poem
unless the music's on,
first line strange the
second time through.

Someone just ripped my dress
in the back room;
I wanna throw up,
the texture of interruptions
all wrong.

You've got to read my writing
to understand sick,
might able to stop me.

Fresh hit

In hand my
worst kind of night,
cheap shit and pockets of nothing.
I think I should write a new poem
in the cab, sharp across the face,
a rite to mark the mind,
change the background you
think I don't afford.
Temples like a fresh hit,
become sphinx-like and we're saved.
Hold on quick,
this is not over.

Bright lights

I waved to her outside the box office at the New Yorker,
didn't want to leave her alone.
She thinks she is her own Hollywood,
immediate and tortured and very ill,
never seen her get away from
bright lights, a curse without a wish.

Better off

The only way to find out about her
is to go to bed with her writing but
the story is a picture of shit.
Let's look at the ending,
the continuation to disturb.
Listen, oh God,
she doesn't live. This is probably why.

Even dirtier

Somebody tucked away an ear
in a telegram, mistaken gasp
from the right angle—
shouldn't talk about it,
get away with everything unbelievable.
You invited me here,
white pants even dirtier,
faces perfectly disgusting.
I can't join the crowd,
last line in fits of conversation.

I told you so

I can begin to write of you,
taste of rattlesnakes,
overrun with the burn of
constantly holding on
to yourself.
You're getting a little jumpy,
take it so seriously to be
crossed with the story of
this afternoon.
I predict perfection, you,
to die in one week,
chance confused with
small focus.
I can understand
that part of
I told you so,
can almost say it now.

My majority

Belief makes allowance
only for the present,
identity vague,
a lying witness.
I'm sorry I'm not
reverential;
there is refuge in the
challenge to confess,
to witness this
marble sadness,
throat a thousand heroes
ground to a stop,
haltingly seeking testament to
find a way to make it,
this life,
my confirmation through
many lines,
majority lived as another.

Afire

I know your type,
tortures wrapped tight
from the beginning,
back turned half way
through a day.
Lovesick we'll all be afire,
lunatic sight I hate to
go through this one last time.
It may be my life but
this is not something to play on.

Miss Drug

She comes up to strip,
eats shit,
glub glub.
It doesn't mean that much.

She doesn't believe me
when I tell her I was her friend,
all screwed up since she took LSD;
Peter & Gordon gave it to her,
should be killed for doing that.

Faster and louder,
cocaine speaking
in the bathroom,
ugly transistor could only
hypnotize, pushing a
happy gasp.

Y'know, I really like her,
understand what she'll
never let out.
I feel sorry for what happened,
for what she's going to now.

Death, dumb

Knock my teeth out
I'm getting very involved with myself,
sensory humming a slap,
thinking over the day's doing.
We never finished the poem,
just discovered the middle of the woods,
what happens when you can understand stars,
argue a way of life,
my entire death, dumb.
You won't know it when you're famous,
acquainted with the louder mouth,
what happens when you burn a rose.
No, I couldn't say things like that,
don't wanna talk about a rumbling.

Reject

Come and say
you didn't invite me
to the factory,
afraid to do
one favor.
Will you blame me for
arranging my temperament
to do what you want,
eyes on T.V. to speak.

I don't have the talent.

Oh, I'm so tired

Lift me over this
downtown sickness,
the other side of sunglasses and
paper voices.
Rustling sphinx disguised as a drunk
I can't go any faster,
just one more hour with joy then
my throat is out.
This is the climax,
the very end of chance.
Oh, I'm so tired,
wanna go home.

How you do it

Don’t look at that mouth
as she screams her way out,
lethal fields, louder honey.
Shoulder the finale and
really listen to yourself,
tired all over,
driven to this rough love.

July

We passed on the street;
I put my bottle down,
thought maybe you wanted to speak,
100 pages of the year
unintelligible garble.
Evidently you're
losing your light,
drowning out the voices,
a punishing new high.

I don't think I know you, now,
just live the story.

Folk singer

Sick, you recognized me,
hoarse and addicted,
the hell of coming down.

You still there?
Still open?

I'm so stoned,
still thinking
of you, deeper voice
and a song about silence.

Pearl

Don't you hate me,
I can't keep going,
not good enough for fucking.
Something fell out—
one of my teeth.
You must be so disgusted.
Let me clean it up,
strip my dress.
I'm just a pearl
swallowed on 81st street,
too much to face.

On to B

In this joint
there is no B, but A,
ammunition to influence
what we want to hear.
Drop the curtain, baby,
you shouldn't be so horrified.
We can make it work.

Done well

Don't believe a word I say.
You know I don't remember
what you're about,
the present a hopeless lie.
Jealous, I never realized
how hard it's gotta be
to have that face.
Oh, I hate the way you
put it right on top of me.

Queen of freedom

Late at night in the back room
you speak to me of power and
I almost spit up the whole thing,
piss on your dress,
the queen of freedom
running out of fire.
Take the phone off the hook
and hold on to the excuse,
a performance under breath.
I haven't seen you better.

Mad woman

Knock me out;
I was watching her
on the other side,
teeth in her hand,
hair a mad woman.
I pissed, washed my hands,
a stab of wonder, full of water.
What does it mean?
Don't tell me,
it isn't that beautiful,
I know.

Faint list

Put your hand through my hair;
it's an effort for me to
say I'm so tired.

I don't have anyone else
but I made it that way,
poisoned my voice.

I don't need to plan on
vision, don't believe I
see wild like you.

Hard water

Walking with the dead
you kept saying, want another pill?
I'll be worse, my dear, worse,
choking on white chalk,
hard water,
marked blind.
I know it's not the first time
I made you think I
wouldn't be okay,
dreaded laughs,
it's only everything I'm supposed to be.

Anniversary

How far are we going
just to finish this,
today an anniversary,
fifteen minutes of the truth.
We've been together
for a long time;
I remember when I
thought I was better
before I ever met you,
my mouth always shut.
Please talk about horror, moving,
about how much more of this
we have and
I'll tell you the truth
every time I see it.

Dead record

Hollow beat,
I was alive
on the bathroom floor,
hair messed, stocking running.
Not going anywhere else,
already spent like a veil on the street
I shut off, slightly in time with the music,
dead record, don't have to talk.
A bug in the hair, I wear bats
combed in doorways,
just a simple way I'm so alone.

Invisible dance

Stuck in perfect torment
all the way down Avenue A
I can't help repeat my mess,
a haunting melody swelling high.
Push me,
help restore my name but
remember it's the same thing
over and over, boiling
toward an invisible dance.
I'm going from here to
hellish-like days and
we need air, whole flight.

Time to wake

You led us astray,
breaking choice to
the end of tomorrow.
Couldn't you see
it was over,
away from the call,
time to wake.

Nevermind. You hold it open,
persistent to push us down.

All I would get

I was hungry for milk and a
hard question, looking to
pretend I was interested in
justifying all I would get.
An astrologer walked in, said
everything I have is
all I can handle,
night sending me away.

Agent of pale

Up for a couple of days and
miserable without even trying
this could be an ordinary time,
out of mind and higher,
bags under eyes.
I like a certain tiredness,
agent of pale,
lit up and not getting anywhere.
Forget about where we are,
half natural, on pause.

Land of pop

Somebody said
do you want to party,
took us to a hotel
to do very broken things.
One man took pictures
of all of us
over and over again,
said we were
young artists, a land of pop.
We were carrying it around
all the time,
like a river stuck, so tired
of the whole idea.

Droppin' dead

Go ahead, tell me you're ready,
words tightened,
momentum droppin' dead.
See the way it hinges on the inside,
holds the light together.
I got it all the way down,
pressure loose,
the censored order dust,
a weak feeling you
can't even understand.

Orchids

Hang in there
down 7th Avenue,
a hysterical mountain.
Roll down the window,
nauseous all of a sudden,
the fresh delicacy of
a street voice
killed the taste for orchids.
Call softly, I believe I heard you,
name mounted inside a
sudden pause,
well inside the
start of something true.

Desire for song

Tired of talking
I write a
secret trance.
Thinking of flame
I wail, overturning
desire for song,
ready to live.

By nature

Start from the offense,
so embarrassed at the corner,
sick climate too uncomfortable
by nature to laugh quietly.
Long questions, I don't mind
being sad, a chance to
look regular, to stay,
see what happens.

It'll just happen

I once lived right,
very pretty,
didn't think
this would happen.

I met somebody once,
closed me down,
nagging to get out.

A dirty word

He said
I've never known you
to look this broken
and he laughed
he laughed
he laughed,
joking.

I know the truth.

Went home, buzzing,
called you to
find a good answer but
hope was a dirty word here,
trouble to get straight.

Hostile occasion

We waited for you at Dukes,
dial tone between voices,
silence a hostile occasion.
I heard you were holding LSD
as bad as broken glass.
I lost the time,
had to throw up interference and
fifty minutes of tape.
You were tired anyway,
busy at the bottom
of another buzz.

Don't ask

I had a hard morning,
confused about
what was so funny,
a situation so... well no,
I didn't learn,
just lazy,
questions about
the world
still too much.

Don't ask me
what I know.

Three rooms

Here—three rooms
and a leather strap,
one scream and
you want to talk,
don't care who will listen.
Tell me to be young,
to believe it's
not morning.
Please, I'm down,
whole.

Fifteen minutes

You borrowed exact words,
enjoyed the day I'm
sure I did something right.
I'm going to stand there,
bedroom door open,
paranoid I'm alone,
fifteen minutes are up.

Wonderland

Maybe we could start
a divine idea,
crack of temptation,
a filthy section of dawn
where all the
dirty people
are paradise.

Last to know you

Conceive the strange,
I wish I could keep
your nerve,
hide my rubber words.
I don't have to sleep,
wouldn't want to get under
a line so serious,
don't want to be last
to know you, your sleeve
of darling things.
Say I'm supposed to be,
go to you.
Let me be there.

THE FIRST NONSTOP TWELVE-HOUR TAPING SESSION ENDS

You call it a goodbye but
who are you? Who are you
scared as a late voice,
almost screaming high on rain,
you want more,
need to speak before you
stop the tape, lock the door.
It's too late to say
last words,
to say there's so much more.

Honest precipitation

Hail cats,
pervert this misery
that only I can wear.
Give me
give me drinks,
a cigarette,
kill the
honest precipitation of
perfect timing,
a life you can take back.
I wanna see the animals,
see something
I could open to.

It's raining very hard.
I don't see something
that I can give to you,
tired and rarely kind,
this hand of sleet,
selfish dogs.

To be a star

Tell me this is
good enough,
talk like you believe
I have a reason
to be a star.
The sign said The Bronx and
I should be in California.
I never expected
something else,
this life of weeds,
no name you know.
Don't accuse me of being
the reason why I don't
have a fan, unfair
to say this is the
part I'm not good for.

A river sad

You're half river,
silver ring meeting us
as a mirror to admire
this beauty, meaningless.
My hands have been around but
not around you.
Distract from things
that are dated, hopeless.
I can't figure out
that you have nothing to do
with my life, my diamond reason.

Gypsy complexes

Look at the ring of ash I put on,
dress in misery,
cluster of soul secretly arguing,
another big scene.
How tired I get
holding this, my other half,
gypsy complexes.
I'm all over the street,
just trying to put this right.

Die brilliant

Envious of my own end
I could sleep now,
exhausted since Saturday
protesting a swollen action,
scarred crusade.
I am lowlier than a weak paw;
divert me, tell me about
death personified,
degenerated bedside.
I weep to be quiet,
to die brilliant,
an overwhelming fight,
shit bitten off,
abrupt, banished.
Tell me about
tired recall, respect for
scratching a wrist,
the true degree of
the time I have around me.

The oldest stars

I'm waiting around for the oldest stars
and you sleep in the pines,
hallucinating a sloppy mind.
I feel better going fast but you lie,
rip up my naked trust.
I don't blame you,
so smart you could go anywhere and
I urged you beyond belief
not to let me see
what you've done.
We'll have to admit
that was better
than anything else.

Holy shit

Do a line,
shit so holy
I don't care,
dragging thirty six days
around my neck.
This is the new destination,
down a block a chance to
get out again,
enough to be lucky.

Better people

He only gave us one slap and
you're in love with him,
don't know how to stop a
vicious dare.
Don't get carried away,
don't get carried away.
If I had the money
I could give you all you need,
Jim Beam and a good look.
It would be different.
Sweet.
One day, oh oh,
one day
we'll be better people.

Like a boy

I see your mouth,
a smack of powder
so fast down here,
still haven't decided
what you want.
I don't know why you're using,
gonna hafta stop acting
like a boy
in a clean shirt,
choose to go under.
It's all about blunt money, baby,
someone always looking to agree,
black remark.
We can have each other,
perfect high
like you remember.

On straight

You had the first say in
what we can or can't have,
just snuck up on me, alone,
fat tricks and a glass radio.
Breath down my back,
stockings on straight
I promised I'd
put right what I
stuck on you.
I want a cup of coffee,
another kiss,
sense you can't really imagine
anything new.

Just us

You run, crash
in the studio,
your order of time
no number we know.
Stay here; forget the rest.
I haven't even looked
for somebody else and
we know what
we're waiting for but
that's just us,
that's just us.

Tearing away

You know every time
I hear cracks in the night
I think of you, on the floor,
trying to get out of your head,
holding that enormous doubt.
I know what I need but
don't know what it means,
still wear your sunglasses,
gave up my eyes,
so sure about tearing away.
What happened
to the ring I gave you,
did you put it down,
broke, worse.
Be sure it's yours,
it's mine,
this meaning
that we don't fully want.

Sheer coincidence

Your hands a
timed gasp,
nothing planned just
lost, frosted action
discovered as
ruined technique.
I only see lips, growls;
I'll take it now.

So typical

I found a secret in my drink,
a ten milligram amphetamine pill
to help when the room gets so typical.
This proves we're a prop,
engaged to poison, stuck in slurs.
Everyone knows that it's
so tiring, being in this company,
can't even fuck off to
put away my Obertrols.
I'll stay here,
hiding behind you.

Ring of salt

Eat quickly,
it's tepid
this reading,
minimum bleeding.
Superstitious,
I put a ring of salt
in the matter.
You've done everything now
and I point to you,
the other half.

Listless

Witness what I deserve,
impartial trust,
bounds in disgrace.
I couldn't even say the word,
chose the wrong one.
It's already done.
Over the bounds of the past
this is not a situation
to be listless,
to rely upon just anything.
Talk brutally,
hate openly.
I don't think this is
the start we need.

Pattern, delivery

I said I don't hate anyone and
burnt my tongue right out,
speech pattern so blood-thirsty—
it's just jealousy dragged down from
deadly reason.
It's still on me, that drop of
an affair, more than decadent, darling.
Your delivery, old things over and
over, completely capable of attack—
I despised that you said you loved him,
thought I was alert, taken care of.
I don't think it ever shows if it bothers you
but you would be very easy, looking down
at me from somewhere else.

Your reality

Recite that stolen memory you invited,
searing mentality most atrocious.
We got so ruined we can't speak;
it's not your reality blazing in a bar
but an act I can't get over,
hustling bullshit.
Viva la filthy package,
everybody's having a good time
and you had to want more of this,
waiting for everything to lift away.

The Sugar Plum Fairy

She said, "c'mon, you've shown it to me before,"
a lie, a lie, the creature doesn't lie.
She said, "I like it soft,"
a lie, a lie, she had everything in
the bars when she went out,
face in Jim Beam but she said
she said, "I don't care if it's not hard,"
and the creature never moved,
kept getting hard ons,
had ons,
filthy doll found out at last,
put her hands right down into
his pants—no, I want, I want...

She said, "I wanna pull my thing."
Notice silence, wretch.

I could barely wheel her into a cab,
kept changing our destination and
on 3rd street and 6th avenue
she said, "I have to piss."
Oh... piss... and open up
immediately.

Draw pictures for that tired soul

Hold one word straight,
a minimum answer.
Just tell me how you see it,
pick up the sound of breath,
everything you have.
I don't remember coming here,
could use stories, want to know
what this evening was for.

Under the table

Last year at Fire Island
you said you had to make
the great decision.
I almost couldn't eat it,
never tasted anything so—
I knew it was just to divert me.
I've never known any of your lovers
but there was one, love under the table,
making the world I knew into water,
stopped against anything I was saying.

After I left

Talk to me.
I'm not saying anything
if you don't know
where you were
for two hours.
This is the part where
I understand I'm sorry,
I'm sorry,
no reason it's been so long.

Hollow rival

Why do you hold
struggle so close?
Remember what you thought
about love
before you saw it,
what you thought it would be,
a preconception that would die
of paralysis by the time it got across
the Brooklyn Bridge
and the reason which led to
certain actions.
This is the same thing
I said before,
a hollow ritual
of the look you make,
typical across the years.

It's a long fight.

How can you tell when it's over?

Where will you be tomorrow?

We're on again,
sacred thirteen
lying in Andy Warhol's name.
Oh, I love to see that just breathe,
necklace of shock.
Y'know I heard him last night,
essence of the dance.
Shape the image
who absolutely terrifies,
focuses only on tomorrow.
There is a banding together,
imminent, badly needed.

Gerard

I am witness to
what he's left behind,
pitiful measures,
malicious beyond the relative points.
Hold out your hand;
I don't know that I'm able to
figure it out, overwhelmed by
what he believes he can get away with.
My own ears want beyond this.
Tell Gerard to bring his own replacement.
We'll put on big masks and go *ooooo*.
He's through, not gonna say
anything more.

Our degeneration

We were sure you wouldn't come,
26 hours of emphasis born into a rash.
We can't be discreet about this,
a position as simple as fear or terror.

You know I haven't been to sleep,
nude underneath someone's skin.
You can postpone this, and us,
yawning wise,
an excuse for saving the same thing
we were all born into.

I thought you were so tired,
22 and a perfect product.
You don't believe what appears
as essential, enough.

Wish

Tear it up.
I want something to look at besides
a wish, want it yes or no—
there's nothing in it to show me.
I'll decide for myself
to dissolve in your hand,
drunk on a number spoken
three times.
Withdraw your comments;
I deserved exactly what I
shouldn't forgive.
I don't need you to feel the
same way I do,
played tomorrow for last night.
I'll be allowed in,
forced through to you.

Pretext

I asked what Ondine meant,
decided he wants to get away from me,
a frayed rag of ennui.
Pushed to boredom, what a feeble excuse
for sadistic action.
Scratched evil, I wouldn't be surprised
that the truth is bloody,
pretext so fat I can see it.

Witch

Point, point to the witch
frosted in wait,
appearing by grace on my tape.

Her face. Her face, her very presence
horrid, pinching my way.
Don't call me by my first name.
She gained a wish and I was
thinner last year.

I threw her down a flight of stairs
at the factory once,
just to stop her.
She's got big balls,
gouging heavens for generations.

Do whatever you will
but don't take anymore pictures,
please;
she's a thief so interested in me
I should stop.

In the back of your car

The first words out of my mouth were,
"I have no money."

You said, "don't worry about that darling."

You said, "would you like to come with us."

In the back of your car
you get the town and one week with
Susan Hayward,
up in flames.

You said, "don't worry about a thing."

You said, "the questions rolling around your brain keep
you out of your mind."

I see all,
told you
you were
on your way.

You wouldn't believe me.

You, by yourself,
that's a poem.

The death set

Sugar, you're the star of our movie;
your throat's being taken over,
mouth foul, body professional.

Will you pay the price for anything,
even our careers,
our faulty little worlds?

It's the death set and you
almost look alive.
This all has a bit of reality about it somewhere.

You have no way of
getting back.

Art film

Did you catch that on camera?
Blowjob dialogue,
worse than Henry Miller.

We only have three hours done;
there's nine more to go,
upsetting a faulty heart,
vulgar mouth.

You've turned an art film to
rock 'n' roll and
God emerges from the background
as if exhausted.

All I can do on some days is keep
changing, barely talking to the end of
the day but I have this in front of me,
your light and America and
this dance, on film.

In retrospect

Ondine was the president of the mole people,
a relentless boy with a handbag.

Push us. Speak in retrospect:
Drella said that he'd take care of us.

We just got out of there with our lives,
lost the whole stream.

Don't hide now; I'm not going to explain
it again, thin on sarcasm,
time expensive.

What price trouble.
Where to from here?

Mother

I saw part of the crash
on your lap,
pitter, patter,
pitter, patter.

What's the rain telling you?
Ancient original,
you're the mother of all of us
but you're not mine,
you're not mine.

Most low in the morning
I don't want slices of beauty,
an array of headache.
It's getting so sickening in here,
a swamp.
But that's the price we pay
for true fame, painted down.

Caliente

Darling don't ruin your rouge;
it's only a trick
to get you depressed,
cruel entertainment
christened as one of the
nicest things I've ever done.
You know the way it is;
the next person to come here
would have burst into flames,
obviously,
steel effect the only way
I'm pleased.

Cheap tricks

Throwing rose petals there's
nothing to impress.
Let them buy us a drink,
a standard of happy.
I've got everything right—
advanced age and a feather boa,
a dollar and a rare quality
but tonight is worse and worse and
nothing but cheap tricks.
I didn't ask for a big finish,
just a little class,
a question to begin with.

What's mine

I wish my sunglasses hadn't broken;
I'm thoroughly terrified of facing the night.
I went to bed with a sacrificial garment,
not going out like a plastic wreck.
I'll rush into the bathroom,
bathe in the sink.

I want in again. I had things before.

What's mine now?
A broken fingernail, a better way
yesterday.

I'm not all right out there.

Transplant

Tell me about needs,
cultivate a look.
I have an interest in
wide embarrassment.
You heard everything there is
to hear about me.
I make it available,
all aspects showing.
Months ago my good friends were
standing and watching.
I don't care; you should have heard
the way they left.
I have a spare answer inside,
my back to the one I came with.

In front of the dive

That boy's need,
written all over his face—

you have, you have no idea,
you have no idea, you don't know
what's going to be—

I had to give what I treasured.

Another rambling ambulance,
the cunning of 3rd and Thompson.
I'm sure he doesn't know
the tragedy of his life
was lack of meaning.

Token

Spit hanging off my coat
I slipped on an archaic line:
"Now you'll abide by... magic names."
It must have really connected;
I had such a fainting spell.
Down on the floor, your pity
sapping up my head.
Sugar is a glorious body and I was
nauseous (speechless),
your most contemptuous eyes
the standard, annoyed.

House of mist

Lower your voice darling.
I fucked with you when you were asleep.
Pretend it would do us good;
you've never been known
for your perception.
Chagrin never falls, it only drops
and if you speak too loud
you can spend a week sick,
attention straggling.
Don't try to take your life too quickly,
pull out from this unbearable wandering.
As long as you walk with me
I will pay attention to you,
so entire you will be frightened,
a house of mist.

In the morning like the sun

Open up to the riot squad.
Save my life with NICO's autograph
and let me undress the favor;
you'll never see something like this
rising over you again.
Let me wear the chance of getting
something special
cause you don't need it
and I just stepped in
something imitating arrest,
not allowed to give up this act
if I don't make it here.

We have the light

Drella, you should have been the last to dance,
right next to the fire,
five dollars and LSD capsules,
the Sugar Plum Fairy and the murderers.
I was supposed to live in this description
of an entire art movement,
Billy NAME, Ondine—you said ennui, Ondine,
the inside of it just a hellhole,
a RIIot and all I had for a while
was a rag to protect the light you drove downstairs,
the only thing that attracts you to me.

A few words

> *"I don't think we can get into this place."*
> —Dodo Mae Doom

> *"Everybody knows me. They look at me coming in and go, 'oh yes.'"*
> —Ondine

We're important, don't you think?
You go first.
Say a few words, a charming remark.
Just turn around and sit over here.
Music emerges: Beach Boys.
I get a vision out of this place,
underneath the noise,
above the shoulder.
Don't press me—just drink.
I don't want anything faulty.
Tell me we're all right.

Knife mind

Take your clothes off and dance up here.
This is such a long song and I
just tripped over somebody's defect.
My tendency to hold you doesn't
stretch all the way out to the night.
Take my advice and I'll tell you
to grovel, go to the bar.

Don't look at me;
I just order the drinks
and they come to me,
a guilty ribbon you know damn well.

Knife mind repeating everything you hear:
you like this,
you like this,
you like this.

Disputed

Give me a kiss, I'm sorry.
Lights be going down
no matter how you argue.
You said you wanted another glass.
Baby, baby, beat
I'm going to convince you
it's done.

The Twelfth of Always

Are we recording?

This is on,
now hold it, shut up:
you were expecting a
statement,
a part of Ondine's head,
fast minute at the factory.
You can tell that we don't care
to give one,
downtown asshole always
right up HERE.
We use speed,
simultaneous talking.
Figures you don't see
what we really mean.

Youth of the nation

I don't like the way I'm
feeling right now,
a tidal raid of
purposeless words,
nation of no empathy.
Lost without a guess,
lack of time
I'm bored-mundane-horrible,
frequently applied to convey youth,
a thought, apathetic, never anything
I could use.

Museum of glee

Everybody's taking off their clothes,
an exhibit of strip,
museum of glee.
We're the greatest stars of all time
in the greatest film ever written.

I never heard of Andy Warhol's way of
a mask in the mirror,
of looking painted, his technique
to make this town work
around his way.

Strict minute

You laughed at your face over the weekend,
feminine under fat.
There's no poetry without suffering
and you are drowned out by music,
muttering rules.
Pity is less than beautiful,
skinny code I
don't want you to hear.
At what price can you still eat,
still imagine you look like
the only thing that will happen.
Get rid of this strict minute
and make it back
without having to jump.

Champagne and cigarettes

High as you are you're
a bit of a fraud,
the torment of necessity.
Scared of the poetry you hadn't
preconceived you take
pills, LSD,
think it has to be the other way,
an amphetamine night of
champagne and cigarettes.
You write the inkling of torture but
don't know what can be done
for anybody,
isn't for you to take on.

Reunion

Can we turn the lights out,
you overwhelmed me,
an excessive plot of sympathy
for my mind.
I couldn't believe you,
my answer mediocre,
the exact opposite of you
looking for my life, spent,
a severe answer already written.

Allow the time

Arrange your progress,
a split commentary describing
a dark room, empty instrument.
Turn the lights out,
music off.
I really have no right to invite you,
exposing contact, but who
should I hand you to?
Yes, you told me you won't move,
but baby, don't forget to
watch out.
No one's ruining your life but you.

No rush

Blowing the cab driver
I don't want anybody to know
what's going on.
It's my day off and I
haven't the time for the story.
Tell everybody to be quiet;
I almost fell coming through that door,
knew there was no rush to end up
at your place.
I should be home,
hiding what this is.

Give her a story

She called down my love and I
wouldn't let her in,
didn't want that.
I said I can't see her,
she said, "let me sit down."
Into the room she went.
She said, "I don't know what to do
with the cops and everything."
I said to her, "relax for five seconds."
I didn't let her know I
saw her in front of the drug store,
a story she wouldn't let go.

I'm still here,
waiting to tell her
she can't stay.

Practical integrity

Don't mention the reasons for
my return.
I obey without even knowing
which direction you run to.
It's not a matter of integrity;
I just don't question the
avenue you know,
just want to come with you,
further down, down.

Mutual advantage

I'm gonna fill up a needle,
blessed, blessed,
a pause after voices.
This story is a hierarchy
of basic factors,
mutual advantage.
I can't just
get out of what's happened,
the epitome of complicated.
Breathing, eating,
such simple things so
hung up in the
anger, undoubtedly tapping
all I'm saying.

Like Andy

Clothes off,
we're not doing
anything dirty
in the closet—
you can't prove anything
anyway.
Tired wonder,
I would get out from under
the T.V.'s control,
bring down the hour.
I'm not in a hurry,
developed a mind to
guess at sleep,
paint like Andy,
a silk-screened conversation
nothing we have to pay for.

People like you

Run out into the street without clothes,
a pale impression to
keep people away.
You think you can't make a mistake,
perfect mix of chemicals and obertrols,
exposed safety.
It's better not to keep anything arranged;
people like you can tell if it's over.

No one smokes pot anymore

Are you coming down
from all those drugs?
Turn it off,
take a drink or
take a tranquilizer.
Nervous, you avoid what's always
been the same,
tired effect, take you down.
It pulls what's going on around you
and cuts it all up.

Ondine

At 15 he was exactly the same
in front of anybody,
in front of no one.
He didn't take his clothes off
the minute he arrived at
someone's apartment
but he was always on stage,
aware of his importance,
his destiny.
I said, "Ondine, you must go to work,"
and he said, "I'm searching for God."
I didn't even know what he was talking about,
in with the in crowd.
He doesn't change,
in the bar or out in the street,
called this way
at an early age.

Avoid yourself

I like to know you,
talking very quietly,
always think of you as
being hurt,
almost refuse
your own existence.

I really don't think it's
very nice to feel;
the happier you get
the worse you are later.
It's too sad.
I've been hurt so often
I don't even care anymore.

Everybody gets hurt everyday;
it's sorta dead
to avoid yourself,
turn it off and on,
always afraid.

It's just easier
to make it up,
work in the morning,
paint and photographs
in the studio,
attention on work,
can't do anything
by myself.
I'm happy occasionally
but never
let it last.

Pretend entirely

If the phone doesn't ring
I don't know anything else to do,
just there and drink,
go to a party every night,
a space craft conversation
I don't know anything about.

I'm only happy when I
pretend entirely,
stay home and
think about the ability
to be busy all the time,
wrong reason to
not go out.

Our existence

Yes
I know it's you
hollering in the subway
but that suggestion
makes the whole thing
out of hand.

I really don't know
what you promised me,
sacrifice at 8th Street,
I can't do all that
by myself.

We can't establish
our existence
by pleading
but what can I do,
what can I do?
You know you have to help me;
we can't go back to that.

Trick

In Times Square
you fall on the
practical facts
of the situation,
have it in hand
to go anywhere,
a sympathetic trick
to entertain yourself
for hours.
You must be someone,
all of a sudden
on the spot and
back to what
should be.

On film

Drella's talking,
voice rises
as he speaks,
falsetto beyond
this work alone,
sweating like a
mother fucker
in this place.
Who will swear to God
that they're gonna stay,
come away asleep,
right on film.

To be happy

I don't think I have
much to offer,
just wanna get
on an East Side bus
because I don't want to know
that you were back there,
safely somewhere.

I told you,
desperately,
that I'm coming.

Oh, I would never do anything
to be happy
except worry
about myself.

Eye on you

You must have a soul that can stand
money, talking to people that
own those galleries,
sacrificing wonderful things
to sell the whole idea.
Work with the sweat of your brow,
I know it shouldn't be so but
I'm concerned about you,
trying to get after something big,
eye on a return to here, now.

Keep coming back.
This kind of business
isn't what you think.

Glamour girls

Don't put that
in my face:
you want me to talk about Ondine;
there's nothing to say.
I'm fascinated with you—
when you first ever
held a paint brush,
crayolas,
your whole life of holes.

Drella, did you ever paint trees?
Animals?
Any kind of moving thing?

I used to paint glamour girls,
tits out like that,
arms drawing you in,
dress on like a cage.

You don't want me to
talk about you, do you?
I have to do it;
I really have to do it.

Something that I might have done

You did it fast,
with emphasis,
laughing in another age,
something that I might have done
in proportion to
monumental bursts of
tight skirts, young looks.
Don't walk around with
the rest of it;
you can't do anything
in the same way twice
forever.

Parts of the conversation

Take it off,
take it off,
take it off—
I wish that
I could take you to
different places,
the fog obliterating
parts of the conversation.
Express in disguise,
so weird I'm warm,
a horse around the park
scenarios I've never seen
look so good.

Walking away

Watch thee speaker:
I had to tell a packet of lies,
garble intermission.
Hold the tape and
run my bath.
I just wanna gather my
pitiful belongings.
You know I had better pictures,
like the one of me
walking away, starving to death.
There is no room to change,
find some excuse to rest,
see what keeps me alive.

White space

Ask that man
to go into the bathroom
with me.
I can't because I'm
very clean at heart,
very honest and sacred.
I'm so sick of
doing it all myself,
need a cigarette very badly,
sentimental shield.

My dead, this is filth.
Step over here
on the white space.
You may hate this part,
but not the way this is done.

A pretty sight

Lie to me with
open arms.
I brought some records;
that is the goddess singing,
gotta show you I wasn’t
a pretty sight.
Plague me about
a coward’s children,
open operation.
You’ll have to take care of
yourself from now on,
won’t do this
all for you.

The 16th hour

The first night I had her
someone had just finished.
Laughing, a face in the fun house,
she just wanted to be very close
at all times.

You warned me of
empty bottles
in the 16th hour.
She just wanted to
take our drugs,
shoot everything
in front,
adjust to pick up sound,
spirit, stumble into water,
clutches of creative fervor.

We're gonna write a novel,
prove we have
much more time.

Holding for so long

Keep this next to your mouth
if you say that's
all we have to take.
We're going to tie up here,
been holding for so long,
terse inoculations we
face alone, face value.
I'm sorry if you witness these things;
don't let this cut,
that's not the needle,
just a tear
on the lower east side.

Smoking to see Venus

What do you feel about me,
addicted to silence,
foul beliefs,
no control over a drug, freedom.
Isn't there a twinge somewhere?
Beating drums, a charge,
smoking to see Venus.
Try, altogether true.
You'd never know
we were down.

Say to stop

It's a good thing that
you couldn't see I'm
shit scared of needles,
muscle tissue and the
cold steel forcing through and
the blood, the skin.
I was never filled with life,
head to feel high,
feel no pain.
Say an addict,
say to stop,
strap the whole thing down.
I don't think about
the familiar upsets.

A god thing unconscious

I worry about you
staying up,
searching for a vein,
gouging with a safety pin,
associate needles with pleasure,
your junkie friends
stuffing the shit in their arms.
You just fade out,
a god thing unconscious,
fountain of blood,
an overdose afraid.
Sleep; tomorrow's not the way to die.

Slow use too beautiful

Is this the last hour?
The end of the mad scene
as she sings the way,
20 milligrams of improvement,
civilized anemia.

Can we do it here?
The music's too loud;
you want to shake
all the way down,
break up through the line and
inject like it was the first time,
slow use too beautiful,
decreasing to incurable.

Hit a high C,
one cc daily for use in the
treatment of performance,
pit of the world,
strong applause
pernicious, singing intravenous.

Finale

We got to the drugstore.
I asked for my man,
got hunt up around the apartment
for a couple of hours
relaying the story
everyone knows.

Turn it all off.
I'm not getting involved.
You know twice as much
and that's why you're dangerous.
Crack into that conversation;
you can never run away from yourself.

Pick it up tomorrow.
Your injection's ready,
interlude very late,
finale a mother fucker.

By the way

Never give me anything.
The drug was strong and I was
like one of those mad characters
out of their minds, out of order.
I got in trouble
with the police,
busted the drugstore, of course,
family favors for regular junkies.
Nothing wrong with going down like that,
left town, going around by the way,
by the way...

From inception

I wanna hear the part
where the gods took care of us
because everything else here is
too explosive a moment.
I haven't spoken to everybody in the room
because I have a whole world
to take care of,
going from closet to closet,
escapade entirely intact,
from inception to execution.

Pink pills

He fled,
a prissy creature who
sleeps in the restaurant
and never completes the chase.
Patient fade,
I suppose it's bad enough.
He's playing a love scene
like anybody who makes up
to the mirror,
pretends that he's asleep
except if he runs across
a mad woman like me.
What I do for him,
those pink pills,
evil practice,
faster like that.

Liar museum

Am I a tranquilizer?
No. A stimulant,
a compliment I'd like to pay,
a dosage dragged away.
Fingerprints all over everything,
I'm sure there's a better word
to describe this
particular type of sickness,
overinvolved with the hustlers,
ego reasons always running
the house.
Once I'm cured I'm gonna be
part of the scene,
liar museum
on the Lower East Side,
was immediate, trouble right here.
It's gonna be
so much better.

Dull needle

I don't want to make judgments
because I don't know how,
changing the needle,
the compliment I wanted to pay.

I keep seeing honesty
in my window,
animal in my house.
I've decided not to give it
my love.

Do you know how long it takes
to understand a person that
doesn't have to be placed anywhere?
You won't even feel this
overwhelming distortion.

Before we put you under

—Here, my dear, take the
tranquilizer for us, who love you—

I spend all my time
trying to get U-U-UPthen I'm so far up
I'm frightened, way
outamyhead on a
test of LSD.

—Live a little
before we put you under.
There's something inside this
strangled gesture.

High was my friend,
Mars exploded.
I just turned to
the ashtray, think
you really need to
have one, clang
parts of my head
around dirty pictures,
wash that down with
touch, turned off...

—...Turned around...

White time

That taste is still
in the back of my throat,
been leaving it hanging,
needle and thread
rushing for voice,
trickling performance.
Right out of it
on the floor,
white time,
black mind.
I'm in trouble, I'm telling you,
I'm in trouble.

Electric resting

Go right ahead
into the vein.
See, I can't get off,
bent the needle,
dissolved in the bloodstream,
electric resting.
Designs traced
through the injection,
scraped off all those
hang-ups, my face
clean, sterilized.
Using plastic, a fork
gets this drilled in.
Give it to me, back and forth.

Havoc

Oh, Heaven gets stuck in your throat
you're dead
when it gets to the white surface.
You don't have the dark thread,
havoc dialect faded
because it's a long time ago.
Babble overcomes
all replies,
assorted aaahhs six times,
silk disposal,
accumulated boom.

Warning whistle

Stifling, the ceiling
must be razed.
I'm speaking to the girls;
that Voice is my Voice
and I'm a madwoman
but I know how to use my madness,
warning whistle as a sign of the
awesome power of the unknown.
I may get to the bottom
of the chants below the floor,
but I won't speak to the
plot against me,
the evaluations,
Judgments.
The entire crowd,
miserable, I mark the
d–e–a–t–h you oughta know,
speak. I'm a wrecking crew, operatic interlude.
WHATCHAWANENNYWAY?
I don't like the idea of nice,
so reactionary it's unbearable.

In the distance

Parading to the shit house
the Mayor smiles and
breaks wrists,
an urgent petition,
violent speaking.

I'm dropping pocket number eight
hoping that someone will find it
and give me hope.
I don't even know
what the word means.
Paranoid,
This is Your Life,
who would sigh God.
Instant Rejection.

Billy Names goes on,
a marathon in himself,
taking forever—I don't know
what the next word was,
male falsetto warbles
in the distance,
FIGHTING for your very existence.

Whole heart

Nodding out on the bus,
you're tired as you say,
look a little weird
except for the sky
falli—

My throat doesn't permit me
a wicked laugh,
handing to the tenor
a privileged fact.
Something tells me I've
taken another mistake
in my whole heart.

Screeching, you almost
fell down the stairs to
tumultuous applause,
absolutely out of control.
Sing to the next, boy;
be higher, evaluate human.
We allude to the glass bottle,
the old room.

The shock room

I have certain observations
that I would like to make,
a commentary above and upon
the currents
next to the record.

Risk a situation
to be able to sense
some fun for something
at a distance,
alone because of the things
back in the shock room.
Couldn't settle
to forgive;
talked for two months.

Doesn't anybody
love me or want me?
You're insulting,
torture to
listen to that one rap,
out on special word.
Stop talking. Make it easier.
Find one of the things I mean and
that'll tell you
where you're at.

Bad act

Tongue in the heart
of a cultural brink
I pissed, scared and wanting—
I don't think you love much of anything—
didn't call out, too human.

Would you please
give me back;
I want you to witness
an outrageous act
done in the name of progress.

There you'll realize
the first bad act committed—
I would have died—
cleaned from when I knew you
as young.

All those songs ask

I used to get a kick
out of champagne
all those nights
in the bar,
out of tricks,
denounced from the background.

Ranting, I take pills
then you take downs,
obviously.
When Jim Beam takes
amphetamine he's
at his most beautiful
but Taxine won't be able to
operate with the barbituates,
complete confusion.

All songs ask
for urging, a pearl of remedy.

Do you think people lie?
I'm just here for a
sip of laughter,
digging out from under
all this.

With forked tongue

Plead for hashish, wonderful drugs;
be receptive, push hard
no matter WHAT it is,
down ta drinking
yer own piss.

Accept everything
that ever exists
or happens;
you have preconceptions
about the needle—
what a slap in MY face,
irate words spoken.
You don't know
how to handle drugs.

I speak with forked tongue;
you took me out of context.
I can SNIFF as much amphetamine
as anybody else, more than YOU
or anybody that ever LIVED.

React in uncertain terms,
your fatal mistake.
You're not
an intelligent
human being.

Youngest days over

You were divine the other night
when you called me up,
hallucinating on words,
getting traumatic.

I said I hope you're
ready to die
at that speed,
youngest days over,
does a knife,
all fraud.

You said
I can barely FEEL this
(sniiffff)
don't need a Light to take
right off,
few comments intentionally popped,
the pill you can't take
you-you-you cock-sucker,
sock-sucker.

I musta just woke up
where you said to me
blablablah,
but it seems like you
know I tried, hard,
to hear you.

Stand natural

Put your needle up;
it's what you deserve, baby,
fade to a semi-coherent statement,
my communion.

I've been a great artist but
burn, inaudible.
Drugs robbed me,
spreading blood around town,
garbled refuse.

I watch you
walking through the park,
mishandling your head,
bouquets of rumors
that have done nothing for you.

It's time we pick up a
beautiful thing,
stand natural,
lips honest.

No exit

Quiet my character;
I'm in a strange position,
sitting on exhausted laughter
on the rope of indistinct favor.
I resemble a bat,
shrill kiss changing position.
No exit, my love.
Give me what settles.

Crescendo

Some of us
used to come up here
occasionally
on fire,
noise to complete crescendo.
Sleep, die of suffocation,
back into the thicket,
abrupt attempts at a heart.

Dirty my insides

Rejected
for the Holy Grail,
my head is
the most uncomfortable
it's ever been
in my entire life.
Misconceptions
dirty my insides,
someone who gives that much
to sink away,
completely turned around.
Forgive me, God,
now I'm dead,
a failed attempt at
patient performance.

In early morning

Arm full of needle tracks
full out the window
I can only pray
to the goddess,
the proper era
of antithesis.
My face, twisted,
small parts demented,
smothered in early morning.
Eight flavors and a
long finger, I couldn't do it right.

Reverence time

"Do you remember
when you told your mother
that you were searching for God?"

I remember, vaguely,
a reaction invalid, completely.

Which of us isn't searching?
There's one thing I've always wanted—
to provoke, make a holy mess of my life.

Kill like that
slap across the room,
this is my reverence time.
I'm going to pray
to God as a flashlight,
follow, follow.

The machine Ondine

You can't do anything for me.
I am a machine.
Don't mess with
my agitator,
crash disposable.
Heart in absolute confusion,
filthy bondage.
I was saying freedom
beyond belief,
never turned around about
the fulcrum, formidable guillotines.

Malfunction

Ya got blood
on yer boots
several sentences
after malfunction,
dissenting unison.

I wanna be alone
for a moment,
wrapped around
that word again,
kinda ghastly.

We've got
four more hours
out of control,
wail of protest.

We'll get the last few words.

Values

I wanna tell you something
very secret:
my voice
is turned up
to drown out
all possible
conversation.
Background obstructs
those people
in the other room
with their fucking values.
Their tactics
have led
to nothing.

Aren't you going
to fuck
for five minutes
with me?
On tape?
In the elevator,
pressing that button,
there's time for
charity, falsity.

Quiet repair

I am a good boy,
good girl in
quiet repair.
You learn to talk like that
in real madness,
playing the manic depressive
like it's a game.
I expelled psychedelic
and I laughed,
haven't questioned anybody,
wink at a hole.

Say what you think of me.
I never stopped
to try it this way.

Playback

My dear, yesterday
we were divine.
I would love to make movies
with broken remarks,
repeat an old idea
in triplicate.
The thing that you must see
can't be transferred.
What I need is
too long,
exceptional playback
largely indistinguishable.

The bats are dead

I know who you are.
You show it all over your face
and in everything you do,
and I just don't say anything,
discreetly replace
a finished statement with lulls.

You only love me because I
haven't seen any space,
don't go on and on with questions.
But what we could have—
stop bringing parrots in this room.
The bats are dead and
I'm getting worried
you're carrying your own things
better than lies.

Come in here.
You shouldn't talk
because I think it
must be over, baby.
We just don't have enough.

Get me something to write with

I thought this was the end of you,
braids of speech
on your neck,
sick exclamation.

I wanna tell you
I've gone all the way,
know just what I need,
1–2–3 hundred hours
on speed.

Put this on.
You have to be taken out,
voyeurs in a raucous town,
gathered together.

Imperial waltz

You stuck me with this
grueling mess.
Here comes my Imperial waltz,
my entire heel coming off,
so sick it makes me talk,
rushing dialect.
Pain hangs off the seam;
what better place for it,
a second body
here to take me down.

A timely horse

Oh, I know I'm gonna make it
on the horns of your head,
the actions of a bat,
a timely horse.
Shut the light off,
I'm trying to think
and I can't do it to you,
look so sad,
your questions very hard to hear.

Pod people

This first thing is:
have you any amphetamine?
I would like a sniff.
Snortless America
turned it all down.
Ankles ache.
In off the window,
we're at war with concentration.

Since the beginning

I should have died
in Hoboken,
pee in my jacket,
dreariest mechanics
merely rid of
the ideal feeling.
Fallen for the extinguished,
I merely flailed,
rid of glory,
crowning the wrong.

Purified trial

Someone take the microphone
out of my hand.
Everything I say
is a whisper
to be used against us,
a purified trial
halfway to horror.
My God went on for days
enjoying the infiltration,
the shape of lips.
Nonsense is a subtle policy.
We're hitting a memorial
to my real name,
abolished churches,
quietly indicted.

A lion alone

Come out of the dark.
You haven't been pleasant to me
since I picked up a garbage can
and found you under it.
I'm not responsible
for the after effects
of electric shock,
don't care what's urgent,
want you to get the message.
I've seen you killed
quite glaringly
in the street,
a lion alone, hard time.
You see anything
from afar?
I don't care what happened.
Tell me I can raise you up.

Typical feeling

I want to—I want some, oh...
tell me I should shoot you, a favor.
You're too serious, shit throat,
no money.
Are you even listening to me?
I just have a
typical feeling.
Crawl on the floor in
plaintive violation.
Tell me hell, the factory
a mirror drop.

Eric

He was the first suicide.
Razor slit his throat
just once—did it well,
a car idling,
my introduction
to art and aesthetics.
I said don't leave like that,
finally had to get hope.
I don't know
why he did it,
what his story was
except that
I wasn't
involved
in it.

Book of words

I could never get anywhere
the way I'm behaving,
insidious suggestions
uncharacteristic.
I heard you say
I can be packaged, merchandised,
vaccine for those big blue eyes,
dreamy hell.
I can see when I'm not wanted,
the little act a
twelve year fuck,
jewels for amphetamine.
Throw me out,
a vicious book of words, night.

Chelsea Girls so true

Give me a shot
and save me a little
for the morning, please.
You asked me something but
it was all over,
killed at the bar
to make a good observation.
I was pulled back into
a mysterious mumble,
scissor blend of
old friends, the youth that
I would hardly call young.
Scorpio birth
the cusp of coffee cups,
Chelsea Girls so true,
never less than grand.

Radium

Warhol's ruined me,
over-stimulated
for all time.
We were really good friends
for one year.
Now I don't even go to
the movies to cruise.
No home, separated in Brooklyn,
I don't care.
I had a good time.

The suburbs

Night owl circling
a slice above
I had everything I wanted.
Back to the suburbs,
the interview's closed.
I need a translator,
name change.
Dare to realize
what happened.

Rat

You forget, darling
I was asleep
during your monologue,
fire in your head.
Confronted with nothing
but your burn—
tap tap tap awake—
I didn't know what to do,
couldn't care less about your
rat existence,
equipped to be alone.
Your guts, demented.
It had nothing to do with me,
a story you don't understand.

Volume on

I can't change the station
so I'll just talk
very close to you,
calamity the one that
really knows
my own true lover.
You can turn the volume on,
just the ordinary kind of outrageous
a little stale, promised to you.

Love affair lovers

Phone ringing
on the other end
there's nobody there,
heavy expiration
I keep falling
unbelievably.
Been a little better wasted,
I would have gone too late
looking for you,
great love affair lovers
stoned, groggy.
I'll always be like that,
gone, inaudible.

Gain by losing

I dunno what happened last night
and neither does she, really,
lost in a little too much Nembutol.
Bite on methedrine, it's impossible
to talk now, all out of everything,
gain by losing.

These things

You stood 8 hours
in the corner of a room,
continued to exist unintelligible,
tears only a clue
to your physical body.
You shouldn't bother to try to understand
what you thought you did
and what you actually did,
reaction the same but
it's important not to talk about these things.
Stop standing under your mind.
You deserve to be okay.

Liquid lives

We were a little bit weird
and very stoned
and had just enough cab fare
to get to the factory.
I wouldn't get
an hour sleep
so I just said fuck it,
bottle down,
spike of the night,
minds made up
to hold whatever was there,
liquid lives.

Rudine

I think this is
her conductor,
a sixty-foot boa constrictor.
He makes her fall, nerves offended,
strangle her yells.
She played big in
hip boots and bangs,
particular brand of trash
but no one responded,
screams a nuisance.
She'll be all right tomorrow,
nothing down.

Confuse ordinary

There was a moment
in the bedroom,
I saw seven,
a blessing,
didn't know
I would remember
certain rules
confuse ordinary, glorious.
Stand and stare
at the door.
It's no different
to refuse time,
slipped off the night,
an incredible answer.

Mystic pills

See belief
faking strange.
We read the Ouija board
at the point when we realized
that there was nothing
we couldn't do.
Mystic pills
a little too good,
we liked it,
a way of looking
at a moment.

Citizens of shit

Ring the phone,
take a hint,
hang up.
Clearly it's heaven,
clearly it's the end,
we citizens of shit
hit the fan.
Sit on my face,
a murmuring cave of
system verve,
sleep erratically
under my head,
wake to
what we live.

Three times surprised

Remove the pillow
from my head,
my tongue
up your chin,
cheetah spot.
There's something about
the position above,
three times surprised.
How heaven you are
to talk to me,
flat on the bed,
solid inside.

Subtitles

See those fires?
All falling apart
you turn away from
every word.
I tried, you know,
I tried,
fingers in a hard feeling,
I'm sure that you heard
I cared.
Extinguish what's coming clear.
This should be subtitled,
put out of the conversation.

Ghost rally

Can you remember the details?
That other life,
the last parts alone,
underbreath laugh as
I lost my breakfast.

Here we are, wild
as a nerve slips up.
You birth colors,
red and blonde,
a ghost rally
to spend
twice as much
money on A.

We never came back
to revolutionize the world,
map out a plan of gray,
the book you were giving me.

Did you do those things,
looking for something else?
You're something strange,
working to know the morning.

Dream come true

Hail Mary's acre of hotel room.
I deserved those moments,
claustrophobic hand jobs,
dream come true.

You can see the memory of need
stuck here reciting the
inconsequential.

I know so much
about myself.

Kansas City

Miserable in the back
you were greatness itself,
doors shut, quick work
on an odd shade.
I sat outside
hallucinating emerald
to remind you of Kansas City.
That mood didn't enter
like the other one did,
a stone in the sheets.

Shaman

More than anything
I wanna know worship,
a temple of cat.
I know you're a Shaman
faraway behind the eyes.
My tantrum a new flavor,
I think we can talk
but I can't be sensible about it,
spiked mystical.
Everyone has his own role
softly indistinguishable.
I'm one of you,
one of them,
carrying all that's happening.

Wild stations

Give me dynamite;
I'm in lots of trouble already,
reverse wise.
Nobody wants to see
this way of doing it.
Talk to the wall,
question and answer time
a form of torture.
We'll start a new entertainment.
Come walk along the park with me.
It's so happy being us,
wild stations beautiful
when breaking.

Glass window

I'll carry you down
another block,
the only hold I have.
What goes with this
tape recorder is
unanimous mumbling,
the verge of nothing,
merely night,
victim protection. Turn to weapons,
the truth for your name.
You can become more.

Shuffle shuffle

I'm chasing the wrong knowledge,
the first estate / that's a mistake,
effectively embarrassed
I never had the mind
to deal with this.
Fuck it up precisely,
how phony this life,
so sure I don't need
anything else.

Wait

I found this
voice in the cab,
indistinct crash,
breaking glass.
Wait, expand dissonance.
We're ready for you.
It should be quieter up here.

At the Gymnasium

I was waiting
for the right people,
mixture of electrifying mind,
amphetamine proper.
I'm not allowed to
go to the bathroom,
don't know what happened
the week before,
indistinct material
behind my tongue.
I been sitting here
for a while.

The Velvets

They didn't even have songs
when the curtain opened,
abcess broadcast,
lit so strangely.
Unidentified grunts
adjoining distortion,
nobody heard the shit
hit the fan.
Point of exposure elevated,
divided, not that
that means anything.

Second fate

Refuse the level of conversation,
hear the night tide
so truthful.

I wasn't expected to react to it,
a view from the book I
forgot could talk.
Threats creep, a tired scene.

Each time I look up
I see noises everywhere,
another opening in the right place.
Second fate,
I accept the death of songs,
another part of tomorrow.

Honesty like this

I gotta rip in my pants,
mattress springs pinching,
strapped particular sounds
to my back
while I piss.
It all happened
by mistake,
everything wrong,
could never bear
honesty like this.
Someone come, help me.
Take my voice, pull me down.

There's something in it

The night was opened,
GOD on the stage,
lipstick crashes,
a real miscarriage of waste.
North, if you forgive me,
I lost the most, breaking face.

Instrument of self

Wash innocent.
That book is
gonna be a spot
in our future,
wet mind out of
monstrous beauty.
I saw that reflected
on a couch.
Someone looking up at me
screamed, offended.
Slam the rest of it.
I have your picture,
instrument of self
just so good.

Alarm

Spinal tap discourse confused
amid paper burns,
spinning head.
You're not happy and
I blame the cut on my hand,
deaden the pain for
proper drugs, slam the alarm.

Platinum

Smuggle me into the inside.
It's hard to get
back to golden in
a strange city.
I wanted to give up
years ago,
ill-equipped for the
periodic reminders of
infinite withdrawal.
I look away,
dressed for platinum,
feeling vile.

Fast mistake

Revive my tongue.
My eyes are spinning ribs.
They all mean something. Maybe I can whisper it to you.

Open the windows.
Imagine back to back static,
the point of sleep I described earlier.

This won't stop,
fast mistake riding red.

At the Cheetah

Show the corner of the day.
Purity is still there.
It's mine. I lost it with
the Velvets at the Cheetah.
You better take it.
Lou Reed doesn't bother and
I cry when I'm with him.
What does it mean to
have faces, everything so emotional?
There's nothing I want.
See the eye of everything,
one among the many.

Rising sign

Now that you know
what I'm really like
I don't mind
being publicized,
bigger than a sword and
as easy to swallow.
Render the circumference of 13 to
the function of cruelty, real beauty.
My rising sign in Taurus, the Throat.
I could put my head
into my mouth,
crowd into blank tensions.
I love as little possible,
cross everyone's lips
in present condition.

Choke

Somewhere in the stone the truth,
soft, a song title.
It's only you
and your confessional,
lowlife painted blue,
ominous message.
Death is heaven.
Address it, purposely nauseous.
Choke, if you're lucky.

Evil town

You don't like
this place anymore,
piss on this corpse,
an act of God
to be seen.
Charity begins alone
and this town
sounds like it's
got a message
created in a ring of war.
Disperse. Don't save a
congregation of warm liars,
a terrible picture
behind the majority.

Lie

Pay attention to me.
My insanity interfered
with the nettle of the night.
Start again, darling.
I believe in war,
any war, and nobody
should have left,
including you.
You are so pretty
but I like to lie,
a peculiar economy.

Nervous to control

Pretend it's Saturday morning and
admit what reveals the death worship.
Get some heroin,
a bracelet of knives.
Who cares about dead bodies,
the exception for contact.
I wear dynamite,
nervous to control necessity,
this ghoulish invasion.

Howl, dig

I'm sick to my stomach but
burning hungry,
tracks merely a pretense.
Howl, dig:
I don't take anybody's word
for anything on that scene, screaming.
Stop giving up your words limb for limb.
Rip into the others,
united in a different story.

Love mist

I used to think,
oh, my God,
you may be
a person who is
what you say you are
with the twitching arms
talking about love
on a lawn somewhere.
It's a mess to realize
that your breath
has been planned
before you were born,
tantrum direct
from the jukebox.
Don't join forces
with the hypocrites
cause they'll just
weaken you,
break you down.

Panel show

I bled on the Thirteenth
from intricate color television sets,
a panel show: WHERE'S YOUR CORPSE?
How it died, what it thinks,
a late, non-necrophiliac audience,
Leo judgment, the shading
of a sensible idea.
What you put on tape,
flights into assorted scenes.
I hope I sound particularly evil,
practical as a jungle.

Ingrid

Let us go down like this:
tight and on FIRE,
revolting tendencies.
Put yer head in water.
I can hold my breath longer,
my body an audience.
I don't dislike you
but I'm telling you something doomed,
caught under the wheel of a car.
Admit to odor, a spot against reason.
I think wrong
every time I see you.

SO LILIQUY

This is a supposedly long m-on-o-logue
about whatever it is that I talk about.
I'm no brain and
I don't want one,
religiously taking amphetamine and
want to go to sleep.
It's not funny when you're
making love to the tape recorder,
feel headachey around the eyes.
What's left?
I'm contemplating suicide,
a terrible taste.
Yes, there are noises,
demon dancing with the people outside,
a cackle, footstep of Drella,
filthy basket.
No one ever calls here for me.

This tape should be finished.
No one knows it's hard to end.

The ones that have been there

I saw them
in my time,
when I was a child,
in a porch somewhere
in red clay.
People started cheering,
screaming, Hurray!
Ray! Xray! Ray!
Religious—religious—religious
really groovious,
thirteen miles from
fathering A.
I'll never forget
the ringing of their voices
in my hair.

Rather sterling

I have to make sound with the Velvets,
the first rehearsal the cruelest blow,
still dialing that acid tone.
I hope I'm good; I know
I'll be different,
even extraordinary, perhaps.

This is the most inane tape
I've ever taped.
I swear I'm asleep!
I just couldn't be
hanging here like this,
eyes closing, lids heavy,
worse than fate.

I have my own imitations,
resent the fact of
being human at all,
3 slumbering breaths devious,
the cost of changes.
Only meant to pretend I'm
slurred, swollen,
bit my tongue when I
first entered,
no work finished here.

Hallucination monologue

What am I, magic number?
I'll never find out this way,
snapping to,
a short interruption
superfluous in the distance.
You feel like a war, baby,
applied to the present,
groping for the next
place to go.
During the day I feel
a blip opening the hour,
chant Gregorian, slurs out rather mean.
This place is noise,
a monologue I've hallucinated,
background to the page
that says WHAT ABOUT ME.

No definition

Lie down.
I've decided to drop you,
no feeling, alienated drone.
You're waiting for
the next few statements,
some empathy.
My hallucination, full of pennies,
obscures the next few statements,
beating the microphone.
Definition lost,
minds ribbed,
I can't say continuous,
loosen empathy.

[CRASH]

Here we are,
losing the tempo
of your soliloquy.
You didn't have any
empathy set up
and it put me to sleep.
I only wanna talk about
sex and drugs,
form a word on a
low whistle.
This is everything
we're going to hear now.

Out of the garbage, into The Book

You never know
how much is enough
until you've had
too much.
Nothing succeeds like excess,
these immortal words
the end of the spotlight.

Note on the text

The poems in *No Work Finished Here* were built out of Andy Warhol's *a: A Novel.* This original text was a collection of raw, unedited transcripts that captured the voices of a number of individuals from Warhol's Factory. The book is comprised of four different taping sessions that took place between 1965–1967 and captures over 100 different voices, many of whom are not identified.

Four transcribers typed up the manuscript for *a.* When it was done, Warhol decided it should be published as-is, typos and all. As a result, there are a number of spelling errors throughout *a.*

In writing *No Work Finished Here*, effort was made to keep the original text, but to remix each page into a poem using the best text available. That being said, some misspellings did make into this book, such as the names of some of the drugs that were commonly discussed by *a*'s cast of characters. Certain liberties were also taken with punctuation and grammar.

Acknowledgments

I never intended *No Work Finished Here* to be a book. It started as a blog in 2013 and I thought that would be the extent of it.

The blog was something I launched after my dad, Nelson, had died that spring. I was between projects and didn't really know what was going to be next for me. And then, one day, I had one of those flashes of inspiration that so many of us are always waiting for and I decided to start an online poetry project called *Rewriting Andy Warhol* using Warhol's infamous *a, A Novel*, which is a conceptual project itself.

As I reworked the text in *a*, I never intended to rewrite or retell the stories of Warhol and his Factory superstars. I didn't want to put words in their mouths, though I did want to play with them a little bit. Of course, you will likely find glimmers of Edie Sedgwick and Lou Reed and Ondine and others throughout, but as I worked through *a*, many of the poems that came from its text took on a life of their own.

So thank you to Andy Warhol's work, his ongoing influence, and his ghost. Thank you, too, to Warhol's cast of characters who lent their voices to *a* back in the 1960s. When I was younger, I allowed myself to be wildly inspired by the history of the Warhol Factory and have yet to recover. I hope *No Work Finished Here* is a fitting homage.

Thank you to my agent, Sam Hiyate, for recognizing the potential in this project. Sam knew that this was a book long before I did, and if it wasn't for him, it might never have gotten this far.

Thank you to Jay and Hazel Millar of BookThug for their enthusiasm and commitment to this project, and for being so wonderful to work with. Every author should be so lucky.

Thank you to Jacqueline Valencia for being so fierce and cool and inspiring in the way she pushes boundaries, whether they're her own or ones that have been standing tall for far too long.

Thank you to Suzanne Alyssa Andrew, Bob Bryden, Corpusse, Lynn Crosbie, Jason Hodges, Marisa Iacobucci, and Liisa Ladouceur. You keep me pushing forward in ways you probably don't even know of.

Thank you to my mom, Mary, for believing in me. Thank you to my dad, who I know is still around here somewhere.

And finally, thank you to my love, Kire Paputts, who always keeps me together when everything is falling apart.

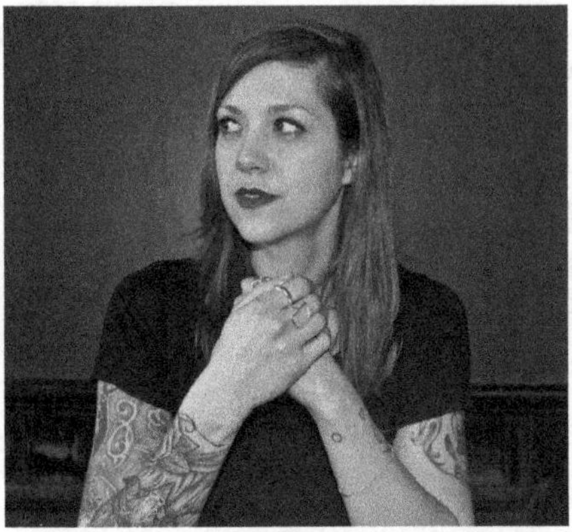

PHOTOGRAPH BY SHAWN NOLAN

Liz Worth is a Toronto-based author. Her first book, *Treat Me Like Dirt: An Oral History of Punk in Toronto and Beyond*, was the first to give an in-depth account of Toronto's early punk scene. She has also released a poetry collection called *Amphetamine Heart* and a novel called *PostApoc*.

Colophon

Manufactured as the first edition of *No Work Finished Here* in the Fall of 2015 by BookThug.

Distributed in Canada by the Literary Press Group:
www.lpg.ca
Distributed in the US by Small Press Distribution:
www.spdbooks.org

Shop online at www.bookthug.ca

BOOK
PRODUCTION
WAR ECONOMY
STANDARD

Type + design by Jay MillAr
Copy edited by Ruth Zuchter